ALESSANDRO CIVATI

BLOCKCHAIN,
AI & CYBERSECURITY

ARTICLES COLLECTION - PART 1

1ST EDITION
OCTOBER 2023
ISBN 9798865158950

COPYRIGHT © 2023
ALESSANDRO CIVATI
LUTINX.COM

L.STAMP

INTELLECTUAL PROPERTY PROTECTION

BY

PREFACE

PREFACE

In our increasingly interconnected world, the growing threat of cybercrime hangs over individuals, properties, organizations and government institutions. The importance of cybersecurity and cyber resiliency cannot be emphasized enough, as both strategies are of paramount importance in safeguarding systems and mitigating the deleterious effects of an attack. Organizations must allocate resources, time and training to minimize risk and limit the repercussions of cyber attacks. Common measures include system updates, antivirus software, employee training, and establishing robust incident response plans.

Cyberattacks pose formidable obstacles to organizations, with ransomware, external resource targeting, and process injection being prevalent threats. To address these challenges, organizations must focus on email security, routine monitoring of external resources, and restricting administrative access. Human fallibility persists as a major vulnerability within organizations, as even the most dedicated employees can succumb to phishing attacks or employ unauthorized devices, thereby expanding the attack surface for malicious cybercriminals. In 2020, ransomware attacks impacted a variety of industries, including education, technology, healthcare, and retail.

Additionally, 2020 has seen a dramatic increase in SSL-based attacks, with vicious cybercriminals exploiting encrypted channels throughout the entire attack cycle. To defend against these dangers, companies must scrutinize encrypted traffic and use sophisticated security tools. Network monitoring is essential to prevent infections and detect aberrant user behavior. Effective solutions must understand the entire attack vector and discern suspicious encrypted traffic without negatively impacting legitimate users.

as we navigate the intricate tapestry of our digital age, the omnipresent specter of cybercrime casts an increasingly menacing pall over individuals, organizations and government institutions. In response to these growing threats, the author has meticulously crafted a compendium that serves as both a guide and a beacon in the treacherous realm of cybersecurity.

With clear prose and consummate experience, the author delves into the multifaceted world of data breaches, exploring their impact on personal, business and financial information, while shedding light on the disruptions they cause to organizations' day-to-day operations. The text examines the unique vulnerabilities faced by companies relying on Software as a Service (SaaS), which are particularly susceptible to data breaches due to misconfiguration.

In this eye-opening work, the author advocates a comprehensive approach to cybersecurity that deftly marries technology with human ingenuity. Readers are guided through best practices to safeguard data and networks, including using multi-factor authentication for administrators, rectifying shared mailboxes, implementing access controls for internal and external data, enabling auditing to improve oversight and visibility, and ensuring that no data is accessible anonymously.

However, the author argues that technological solutions alone are not enough to fight cyber threats. Instead, organizations must also adopt a human-centered approach to cybersecurity by fostering a culture of security awareness and providing frequent and timely training. By doing so, you can promote positive behavior change, reduce risk, and strengthen defenses against the relentless onslaught of cyberattacks. Here we deftly navigate the labyrinthine complexities of cybersecurity, giving readers unprecedented insights into the union of people, processes and technology that is the bulwark against the myriad challenges posed by our interconnected world. Armed with the wisdom imparted here, organizations will be better equipped to address and thwart the ever-evolving threat of cybercrime.

In an era marked by the COVID-19 pandemic, remote working has become the norm, exacerbating cybersecurity challenges for organizations around the world. The author of this book addresses the impact of these changes on the cybersecurity landscape, offering invaluable guidance for dealing with ever-evolving threats.

the author examines the increase in both the frequency and sophistication of cybersecurity incidents, including DDoS attacks and email threats. He points out that remote working presents companies with risks such as unsecured home Wi-Fi networks, phishing attacks, weak passwords and vulnerable personal devices. To overcome these challenges, the author suggests that organizations reevaluate their cybersecurity strategies, embracing collaboration between business and IT security personnel, secure access points, simplified administrator rights, improved technology infrastructure, increased awareness and training information technology and structured data backup strategies.

This talk also emphasizes the crucial role of human beings in cyber security, often considering the weakest link due to mistakes and misconduct. To effectively change employee safety behavior, the author proposes robust, human-focused safety programs that address these issues. Key elements include understanding the factors that influence employee safety choices, providing impactful safety education and awareness training, and developing metrics to measure behavior change.

Exploring how cybersecurity has become a strategic driver for business, requiring proactive organizational transformation and a robust corporate culture, business leaders need to engage in cybersecurity discussions and collaborate with security teams to protect customer data and generate trust.

But we also see here how cybersecurity has become a strategic driver for business, requiring proactive organizational transformation and a robust corporate culture. Business leaders must participate in cybersecurity discussions and collaborate with security teams to protect customer data. and generate trust.

The reflection focuses on the importance of cybersecurity for small and medium-sized enterprises (SMEs), often targets of cybercriminals, and on the delicate balance between the protection of critical infrastructures and sovereignty with the need for personal privacy in cybersecurity legislation.

We will therefore be able, by reading, to have a comprehensive and in-depth overview of the challenges and solutions in the field of information security, providing readers with an indispensable guide for dealing with threats in an increasingly interconnected and technology-dependent world.

As cybersecurity threats continue to evolve, the book guides you through the emerging trends that shape the cybersecurity landscape. Among these trends, the author explores the evolution of ransomware, automated spear-phishing attacks, zero-day attacks, remote workforce targeting, cryptocurrencies, and IoT technology. The author emphasizes the importance for businesses to take advanced security measures to protect themselves from these threats.

The analysis addresses the global cybersecurity skills gap, which narrowed from 4 million to 3.1 million in 2020. Despite this reduction, the skills gap puts organizations at risk in the face of cyberattacks. The author argues that companies need to focus not only on technology but also on training security professionals to better deal with cyber threats.

The author also addresses the new challenges posed by remote working, which put pressure on small security teams. To overcome these challenges, the author suggests a number of recommendations, including accepting that you can't do it all yourself, speeding up incident response through automation, building and training employees on enterprise device management best practices, pay attention to the security of supply chains and adapt quickly to evolving threats, such as ransomware.

You will examine the importance of having robust and up-to-date cybersecurity plans to deal with different threats, such as brute force attacks, phishing and ransomware. In the event of an incident, it is essential to contain the attack, assess the situation, communicate with stakeholders and learn from the experience to improve future security.

But the discussion will also cover the importance of layered protection in the cybersecurity landscape, emphasizing the need to adopt encryption and data protection methods at all layers of the TCP/IP stack. Security must be built into software development, involving both developers and security teams in implementing protective measures.

The overview will be comprehensive and in-depth, both relating to the challenges and solutions in the field of information security, providing readers with an indispensable guide for dealing with threats in an increasingly interconnected and technology-dependent world.

As the exploration continues, attention turns to the opportunities and challenges posed by the advent of 5G and artificial intelligence in numerous sectors such as energy, healthcare, logistics and defence. Throughout the pages, the author highlights how 5G can radically transform our world, but at the same time poses significant challenges for cybersecurity.

The author discusses emerging threats in detail, including increased attack surfaces, IoT-based DDoS attacks, vulnerabilities in network equipment, and privacy issues. It focuses on advanced security solutions, which need to be scalable, automated, and powered by artificial intelligence and machine learning to effectively address these challenges.

During the work, the peculiarities of the 5G network will also be examined, such as network slicing, and the potential implications on IT security. Propose a collaborative approach between working groups, standardization bodies, network operators and vendors to address the security challenges of network slicing and ensure the protection of data and infrastructure.

The author then devotes a section of the book to the impact of machine learning on companies and industries, illustrating how this technology can improve efficiency and address complex challenges. Emphasize the importance of machine learning in handling massive amounts of data, automating manual tasks, and uncovering hidden patterns in data.

It will then analyze the role of artificial intelligence and machine learning in cybersecurity, offering a proactive approach to combating cyberthreats. Analyzing data and risky behavior helps identify potential threats and suspicious activity, protecting businesses from increasingly intelligent and powerful threats.

The intervention thus represents an indispensable guide for understanding the challenges and emerging solutions in the field of information security in a world dominated by artificial intelligence and 5G technology. Through rigorous and in-depth analysis, the reader will gain a clear view of the trends that are shaping the future of cybersecurity and the strategies needed to successfully address them.

Everything here stems from the brilliant analysis of the author who traces a fascinating path through the evolution of facial recognition and artificial intelligence in 2021. Against this backdrop of rapid technological progress, deep learning, expanding markets and moral and ethical dilemmas, the author explores the implications of these innovations and the resulting implications.

The author insightfully examines developments in the field of facial recognition and the growing concern about privacy and misuse by law enforcement. Furthermore, the work highlights the role of governments in the regulation and development of AI, paying particular attention to monopolization and privacy issues related to large companies such as Google and Amazon.

The book also addresses the impact of AI on humanity, examining how machine learning can influence human choices and the moral implications of judgments. The author highlights the importance of interdisciplinary collaboration and policy influencing to improve algorithmic governance and address social inequalities.

Furthermore, the game-changing potential of blockchain technology in the financial sector, food industry and education is explored, highlighting the benefits offered by solutions such as Blockchain-as-a-Service (BaaS), cryptocurrencies, NFTs and cross-chain.

Through rigorous and in-depth analysis, the reader will gain a clear view of the emerging trends and challenges in the field of facial recognition and artificial intelligence. This work offers an indispensable guide to understanding the complex dynamics that are shaping the future of technology and society, and the strategies needed to successfully address them.

In conclusion, we can state that the future of blockchain technology largely depends on its regulation. To thrive, it is essential to strike a balance between the laws and the decentralized nature of this revolutionary technology. Regulators and innovators must work together to create an enabling environment for blockchain to reach its full potential.

The industry must face with determination the environmental

challenges related to the energy used and the e-waste generated, adopting more sustainable mining models and renewable energy sources. Some newer cryptocurrencies, such as Cardano, Stellar, Nano, Hedera Hashgraph and Gridcoin are already using renewable energy and alternative validation methods to reduce their environmental impact.

To ensure a sustainable and environmentally friendly future, it is essential to develop green solutions based on new energy and operating models. Only in this way will it be possible to combine the promise of a more efficient and interconnected world with the protection of the natural resources that sustain it.

Through this work, therefore, the author offers a complete and in-depth view of the challenges and emerging solutions in the field of facial recognition, artificial intelligence and blockchain technology. With a forward-looking perspective and a clear understanding of the ethical and environmental implications, the reader will be better equipped to navigate the ever-changing landscape of technology and its intersections with society.

1
BLOCKCHAIN,
AI & CYBERSECURITY

CHAPTER ONE

CYBERCRIME VS. CYBERSECURITY

Cybercrime is increasingly becoming a threat in today's world. Cybersecurity is a great concern but also a great challenge for everyone: individuals, companies, organizations in general, and government institutions.

Specifically, cybercrime refers to criminal activity using a computer, computer network, or networked device. As cyberspace has grown exponentially, cybercrime has kept pace. More and more cybersecurity incidents are being reported every day, hence the need to do more to deter these crimes.

In fact, all cybercrime incidents are classified into three main categories:

1.1. Cybercrimes against individuals- exploit human characteristics of naiveté and greed. Examples include credit card fraud, child pornography, identity, harassment and defamation, invasion of privacy, spoofing and email fraud, cyber extortion, and password sniffing.

1.2. Cybercrime against property- mostly perpetrated against intellectual property and installed systems. Notable crimes include intellectual property piracy, cyber vandalism, malware

distribution, financial and corporate data theft, web-jacking, ransomware, cybersquatting, crypto-jacking, and cyber trespassing.

1.3. Cybercrime against government/companies/organizations - consists of the use of cyberspace to threaten the government or steal critical economic information. Some notable crimes include cyber espionage, denial of service (DoS) and distributed denial of service (DDoS) attacks, malware attacks, network intrusions, and cyber terrorism.

On the other hand, cybersecurity refers to the ability of a company or organization to safeguard its systems and prevent growing cyber threats. There is also "cyber resilience", which refers to the ability of a company or organization to mitigate damage to its processes, procedures, and reputation and to resume operations after its data or systems have been breached. Building cyber resilience requires adversary threats (from hackers and other malicious actors) and nonadversary threats caused by human error.

In general, the difference between cybersecurity and cyber resilience is not very marked. However, resilience is about accepting that all cybersecurity solutions may not be perfect and protect against all possible cyber threats. This explains why a company or organization needs both cybersecurity and cyber resilience.

Thus, a cybersecurity strategy is needed to minimize the risk of attacks on their networks. On the other hand, a cyber resilience approach will help reduce the impact of a cyber attack. Cybersecurity strategies include measures such as:

- Ensure that all devices are running on the latest firmware;
- Run up-to-date antivirus/malware software, VPNs, and firewalls;
- Providing that all software and tools are fixed with the latest patches;
- All business employees are educated about potential cyber threats

and how their actions can help defend the organization.

Cyber resilience strategies are not as clear-cut and vary from organization to organization. The general rule of thumb is to identify where cyber events and incidents can have a detrimental impact on the company, particularly where the most sensitive and valuable data is stored and used. This provides insight into how core functions can be affected by an attack and how service continuity can be disrupted. A reliable cyber incident response plan will help organizations establish a response team with representatives from each department. The response team will be responsible for notifying them of an attack or breach and then coordinating a rapid response to stop the attack.

Obviously, both cybersecurity and resilience require investments in training, time, and resources from the organization. These investments to protect an organization from cyber threats are paid back in due time, when the organization fends off or recovers from a cyber attack.

2

BLOCKCHAIN, AI & CYBERSECURITY

CHAPTER TWO

THE TYPES OF CYBERCRIME ATTACKS

Before delving into the solution, it is only fair to analyze the problem and get an overview of what the types of cybercrime attacks might be. Here are descriptions of some of the most famous cyber attacks.

2.1. RANSOMWARE ATTACKS

Ransomware refers to that malicious software that blocks access to a computer, encrypting the data it contains, with the goal of obtaining a ransom from the victim in order to gain access to their data again. In 2020, there was a sharp increase in the number of ransomware attacks. No business sector has been spared from the tentacles of malicious cyberspace predators. Ransomware actors often gain access to a targeted corporate network and steal data by encrypting it. Their actions cripple the company's daily operations and demand ransom. Not only that, some groups threaten to sell or expose sensitive data on the Internet.

Reports from cybersecurity experts reveal that ransomware attacks increased by about 30 percent of all cyber attacks in 2020. Among the

most viewed ransomware variants were Maze, Ryuk and Sodinokibi. It is expected that with the increasing number of ransomware attacks, all types and sizes of companies in all industries will be impacted. According to my research, these are the 5 most common ways organizations are targeted by ransomware attacks:

1) Email Attachments
E-mail is still the largest attack surface in organizations. Every organization relies on email to communicate. A concerted effort is needed to address email attacks holistically and boost email security. Many attacks start with a simple email attachment that executes malicious code and spreads a ransomware payload throughout the organization within minutes. In most cases, the attachment can be a JavaScript file or a ZIP file. These files are popular email attachments and allow attackers to easily introduce malicious code and execute an organization-wide attack.
An effective way to prevent ransomware email attacks is to evaluate all incoming emails and identify the most common attachments. For most organizations, the most common attachments are Word documents and Excel files. In this case, all other attachments should be blocked and processed as needed. Exceptions can be made to ensure that non-typical file types can be handled differently as needed.

2) External Facing Assets
There are two types of externally-facing assets: intended and unintended. There are specific assets, such as Remote Desktop Protocol (RDP) or Server Message Block Protocol (SMB), that are particularly vulnerable to attack.
Both intended and unintended assets are targeted for attack through

existing vulnerabilities and brute force attacks. Unintended assets present the most significant problems for security teams because they should not be exposed.

Companies need to have a thorough understanding of their externally-facing infrastructure and take steps to identify infrastructure changes or suspicious activity. The ideal scenario is to use a third party to audit all of the organization's outward-facing assets, such as solutions developed to help internal teams determine all assets that appear in the public IP address. This information should be collected and reviewed regularly to keep track of any changes. Institute measures to ensure that user accounts that attempt numerous logins are locked out. The most critical charges to protect are service accounts, which generally have more privileges than end-user accounts. Server accounts also have back-end configurations to automatically reset access attempts or disable lockout policies that can disrupt business operations.

3) Process Injection.

Process injection involves the execution of arbitrary code. Malicious actors use process injection to introduce arbitrary code into normal running processes. For example, TrickBot uses the legitimate svchost. exe file to inject and execute arbitrary code and eventually take control of a corporate environment.

Process injection relies on stealth to mask attacks and make them difficult to detect. The use of stealth is such that malicious processes cannot be seen when examining processes running on a host.

The execution of arbitrary code depends entirely on the user context in which the processes are running. A legitimate executable run by a signed user is different from an executable run by a system administrator account. The solution is to remove as many administrative rights from end users as possible. Reducing administrator access reduces the success rate of arbitrary code execution.

When an endpoint is compromised or suspicious activity is suspected, it is necessary to identify all legitimate executables that could perform anomalous actions. Using the example of svchost.exe, check whether the process establishes a connection to a remote IP address without a command-line argument.

4) Inventory Asset Management.

A major challenge for incident responders is to fully understand how incidents affect core business operations. In addition to possessing the necessary technical skills and keeping abreast of the latest tactics used by attackers. Small businesses have to deal with small or even nonexistent cybersecurity teams, while large companies have to deal

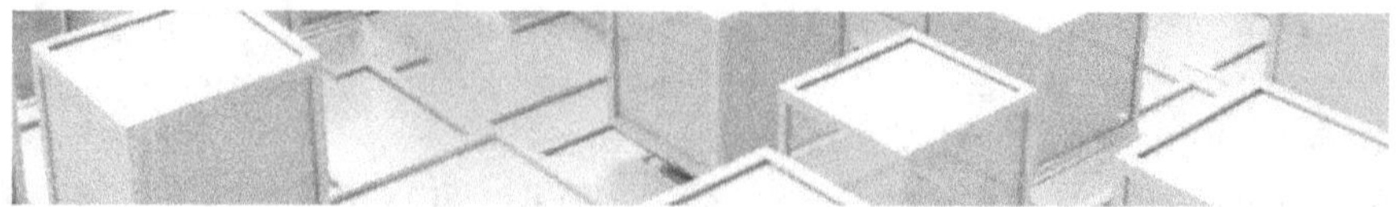

with numerous assets and more infrastructure.

During incident response, visibility into more infrastructure will provide a more meaningful opportunity to detect anomalies. Attackers have gained the upper hand when an asset is not properly monitored by security teams. Repeated damage has occurred when numerous environments have recovered from ransomware attacks only to be compromised a second time because preventive policies were not in place for all endpoints. In some cases, security teams were unaware of the existence of endpoints and malicious actors compromised them. Asset inventory management requires organizations to be inflexible in understanding their environments and all assets. Security teams can use inventory management software or integrated tools such as PowerShell to regularly gather information and ascertain the status of each purchase. Inventory management is an endless process characterized by continuous learning and monitoring changes.

5) User/Human Error

Human error is the weakness of organizations, even when they have the best security team and the best security tools. Many attacks begin with an employee opening an email attachment that allows actors to gain access. Even the most diligent employees can fall for phishing attacks.

Watch out for devices that are not registered but are used to connect to the organization's network. These devices and apps increase the attack surface exploited by malicious actors.

Another research of mine, reveals instead the sectors most targeted by ransomware attacks occurring in 2020, such as:

- The Education Sector. It was the top market for ransomware attacks, with schools, colleges and universities. In almost all cases, threat actors demanded ransom from victims in cryptocurrency, especially Bitcoin. Failure to honor the ransom demand could expose students' stolen data.

For example, the College of Social and Behavioral Sciences (CSBS) at the University of Utah paid a ransom of $457,059.24 to attackers who had gained access to their computer servers and the encrypted data they contained. The attackers fulfilled their end of the bargain by providing a decryption key for the stolen data.

The U.K.'s National Cyber Security Center has warned educational institutions of the growing number of ransomware attacks against them. For the record, in 2020 alone, more than 86 colleges and universities and more than 1,224 schools experienced attacks that disrupted operations. Educational institutions must be vigilant and take measures to protect against these attacks. The Cybersecurity and Infrastructure Security Agency (CISA) and the Multi-State Information Sharing and Analysis Center (MS-ISAC) in the United States have pointed out that DDoS attacks, malware and ransomware are the main threats to educational institutions in 2021.

- The Information Technology Sector. Following adjustments to the impact of the coronavirus pandemic, the information technology sector experienced several attacks in 2020. Most business organizations bore the brunt of these times, adapting to distributed networks as employees work from home and must defend against sophisticated attacks. Ransomware attacks have been rampant, targeting large organizations that are more likely to pay ransom to attackers. The average size of ransoms demanded increased by about 33 percent in 2020 compared to 2019.

- The Healthcare Sector. A more worrisome trend is the increase in the number of attacks directed at hospitals and other healthcare facilities/provideries. Ransomware attacks against the healthcare sector have sought to steal and exploit valuable medical data and other resources. There have been attempted attacks directed at research information for the development of a COVID-19 vaccine and its distribution to hospitals.
In the second half of 2020, a series of Ryuk ransomware attacks hit several hospitals in the United States.
Cybercriminals managed to compromise the critical network systems of six different hospitals in a single day, causing widespread panic throughout the industry over the theft and exposure of sensitive medical data.
The Cybersecurity and Infrastructure Security Agency, the Department of Homeland Security (DHS) and the FBI have jointly issued a red alert to all healthcare providers and facilities in the United States for the growing number of cybersecurity incidents. A survey revealed that the number of data breaches in the healthcare sector increased by 2,733 percent between 2009 and 2019 in the United States alone. This also translated into about 1.4 breaches per day that exposed about 500 records per day.

- The Retail Sector. The retail sector was not spared from the increase in the number of attacks in 2020. E-commerce has been an area exploited by malicious actors seeking critical data and significant ransom payments.

Worldwide, ransomware attacks have increased significantly. John Wick, a group of malicious actors, demanded a ransom for decryption keys after gaining unrestricted access to a database belonging to Paytm Mall, an e-commerce unit of Paytm, the Indian payment solutions provider. They encrypted the company's data and demanded a ransom with the threat of making the data public. Reports indicate that cybercriminals used a backdoor (Adminer) on the company's website to access Paytm Mall's production database and compromise all accounts and related information. However, Paytm denied that its data was compromised and stated that all critical data is intact and protected. Between 2015 and 2020, India experienced more than 1.45 million ransomware attacks, which included hacking incidents, data breaches, and a variety of other security incidents.

In conclusion, ransomware actors have become stronger in their nefarious activities and demand higher ransoms. The use of cryptocurrencies has seen criminals openly demanding huge ransoms, knowing that government agencies will have difficulty tracking the payments. These cybercriminals have found other new sources of revenue, including auctioning stolen data on the dark web if they do not receive the ransom payment within a specified period. Regarding ransom payment, organizations find themselves in difficult situations where they are damned if they do and damned if they do not. Many governments have criminalized ransom payments to cybercriminals because it only encourages them and the funds can be used to finance other criminal activities and terrorism. In addition, exposure of compromised personal data attracts large fines from authorities for the affected organization. Companies and institutions need to implement robust cybersecurity measures to keep malicious actors out.

2.2. MALICIOUS SSL AND ENCRYPTION ATTACKS

According to research by Zscaler, malicious SSL attacks increased by 260% in 2020, including a rise in encrypted attacks, such as a 500% increase in ransomware attacks. On the positive side, the use of SSL and TLS to launch attacks is recognition that legitimate websites and system traffic are encrypted.

The Secure Socket Layer (SSL) protocol has been around for more than 20 years. With the widespread adoption of the World Wide Web came the need to guide and protect deeper online interactions.

The development of a standard to protect communications was necessary and timely. Attackers exploit SSL to launch hidden attacks. The use of encryption now poses a significant threat to businesses and organizations as criminals use industry-standard encryption to evade detection and carry out attacks.

Like all other popular trends or widely used technologies, there are always efforts by criminal elements to exploit the technology through security threats. The SSL protocol has not been spared and thus has suffered a large number of vulnerabilities and attacks. Some attacks have been highly publicized, while others have occurred under the radar.

Because of the increasing exploitation of vulnerabilities, users have been forced to upgrade or move to newer, more secure versions of the protocol. In other scenarios, users have been forced to migrate to Transport Layer Security (TSL), the replacement protocol.

Malicious attackers are finding new ways to take advantage of the widespread adoption of SSL. There has been a new wave of malware in which SSL is being used to hide and further complicate the detection of attack traffic at the application layer and within networks. According to Deepen Desai, CISO and vice president of security research at Zscaler, cybercriminals exploit encrypted channels throughout the entire attack cycle. In the initial delivery phase, there are compromised sites, emails with links and malicious websites using SSL/TLS. On the other hand, payload delivery involves payloads hosted in cloud storage services such as AWS, Dropbox, and Google Drive.

The ability to hide malicious traffic within legitimate traffic means that attackers can advance in the early stages of an attack undetected. It becomes even more difficult to differentiate legitimate from malicious access when the attacker's toolkit exploits existing system services. Some attackers use encryption modules provided by popular operating systems and cloud storage systems, such as GitHub, Pastebin, or S3 buckets, making detection difficult. In other cases, attackers have used SSL encryption on port 443 to export data from specific targets.

Companies should install and use inspection certificates on all endpoints to facilitate SSL inspection. However, companies need to understand that decrypting and reading outbound traffic is only one step to protect against these attacks.

Inspection of encrypted traffic is a critical component of any defense strategy. However, conventional security tools, such as next-generation firewalls, cannot provide the capacity and performance needed to

effectively decrypt and inspect traffic. Because inspection of all SSL traffic can severely compromise performance and productivity, most organizations allow encrypted traffic without inspection, especially if it comes from trusted cloud service providers.

Failure to inspect all encrypted traffic makes the organization vulnerable to phishing attacks and hidden malware, with devastating results. Inspecting all encrypted traffic may be too burdensome a task for the enterprise. Thorough examination of TLS/SSL traffic presents some obstacles that must be overcome, including legal and data privacy requirements.

A good place to start is to use internal DNS systems to implement your network policies. The DNS system will help segment the network based on usage profiles and access privileges. For example, segments dedicated to cloud-based storage systems can be restricted only to machines with legitimate cloud storage access requirements.

Companies should focus on network-based detection, which is both a layer of protection and an opportunity to prevent infections and detect abnormal user behavior.

SSL attacks are becoming popular because it only takes a small number of packets to complete a denial of service attack on large enterprises. The choice of SSL is based on the fact that a single SSL session handshake uses 15 times more server-side resources. The effect is that the attack increases in size exponentially without having to add more bots or bandwidth. The amplification capability causes small attacks to have crippling damage. Other SSL-based threats may include:

- Encrypted SYN floods: The attacks are quite similar to unencrypted SYN flood attacks in that they consume and exhaust resources by completing the SYN-ACK handshake. The distinguishing feature of these attacks is the encrypted traffic and the forced use of SSL handshake resources, which complicates the challenge of IT security teams.

-SSL Renegotiation: The attack initiates a normal SSL handshake and immediately starts renegotiating the encryption key repeatedly to exhaust server resources.

- HTTPS Floods. Usually part of a multi-vector attack campaign that generates a number of encrypted HTTP traffic bugs. Encrypted traffic poses a significant challenge for attack resolution.

- Encrypted Web Applications Attacks. Another trend in multi-vector attack campaigns is to move to logical attacks on Web applications. These non-DoS attacks, when encrypted, go undetected, causing significant damage.

The real challenge with the increase in malicious use cases of SSL encryption is that many of the available DDoS attack protection measures are insufficient. General protection against DDoS attacks is specific to one type of attack. Effective solutions must provide complete coverage of the attack vector and be highly scalable to meet ever-expanding demands. SSL and TSL protection must be supported by identifying and isolating suspicious encrypted traffic without affecting legitimate users.

2.3. DATA BREACH

Rapidly changing circumstances in the IT and business worlds have increased reliance on data and analytics. Data analytics is now critical to how companies can capture new value. The Identity Theft Research Center (ITRC) reported a 17% increase in the total number of reported data breaches in 2020. Major data leaks and cybersecurity breaches were reported in 2021.

Specifically, in 2021, about 281.5 million people were affected by a data breach. There were 160 million victims in the third quarter, compared to 121 million in the first and second quarters. The total number of victims is still 30 million lower despite the increase in the number of incidents. By comparison, a record 2.2 billion people were affected by data breaches in 2018.

Here, there are some data breach incidents that happened during 2021.

In January, Bonobos, the men's clothing store, suffered a massive data breach that exposed the personal information of more than 7 million customers, including about 3.5 million partial credit cards. The hacker group, ShinyHunters, leaked a 70 GB SQL file containing various categories of data that could be of interest to threat actors.

Pixl, the online photo editor, suffered a significant data leak that is believed to have been perpetrated here as well by the notorious hacker, ShinyHunters. A dark web hacker forum exposed more than 1.9 million user records, including usernames, email addresses, passwords and locations.

During March 2021, four zero-day exploits were discovered on Microsoft Exchange on-premises servers. The exploits gave the attackers complete access to the emails and passwords of the affected servers. The attackers also gained administrator privileges on more than 250,000 servers. The installation of backdoors allowed attackers to access vulnerable servers even after making updates to the original exploits.

In April 2021, a hacking forum user published the personal data of more than 533 million Facebook users. The stolen data included Facebook IDs, full names, phone numbers, birth dates, locations, and email addresses of users from different countries. This is not the first time Facebook has suffered such a data breach. In 2019, the phone numbers of millions of users were stolen and leaked.

In May of that year, an attack on Colonial Pipeline, a U.S. pipeline system between Texas and the southeastern U.S., resulted in the theft of more than 100 GB of data and the disruption of a critical oil supply chain. Colonial Pipeline was forced to shut down pipeline operations to contain the attack on the computer equipment that operates the pipeline. The company paid a $4.4 million ransom to Darkside, a hacker group.

In June, the data of more than 700 million LinkedIn users were offered for sale on the dark web. The hackers had collected data that included full names, e-mail addresses, usernames, phone numbers, social media accounts, and personal and professional experiences. LinkedIn denied that it had suffered a data breach and assured users that no private data had been exposed.

And then, in the summer of 2021, in August, Accenture confirmed that the data stolen from its systems had severely impacted its systems and operations. The LockBit ransomware group had stolen more than six terabytes of data and demanded a $50 million ransom. During the same period, T-Mobile also admitted to a massive data breach affecting more than 40 million customers. The admission came after news emerged that hackers were planning to sell a large database of T-Mobile's customer data. According to T-Mobile, personal customer data was stolen, but no financial details were leaked. The attack was attributed to a sophisticated cyberattack.

Lastly, a hacker group, Desorden, breached Acer's servers and stole more than 60 gigabytes of sensitive data. The hacker group first reported the data breach, which was later confirmed by Acer. The stolen data included customer names, customer phone numbers, and company financial data.

Dedicated challenges to data breaches include companies' reliance on SaaS applications for various organizational functions, including marketing, file sharing, and collaboration. This widespread adoption, however, has identified a possible vulnerability and that is the lack of resources to properly configure applications to avoid cyberattacks, data breaches and other cybersecurity risks.

In fact, SaaS security configuration errors have been blamed for costly and devastating data breaches. Misconfigurations have often led to inadvertent exposure of file systems and databases on the cloud service.

Every company is as vulnerable as some of the weakest settings it has for its SaaS applications. Security experts have come across localization errors that make companies susceptible to data breaches and corporate espionage at the click of a button. Many companies have exposed the entire cloud because of simple mistakes.

Here, there are the most common SaaS configuration errors that you need to check and eliminate to protect your data and networks.

- Ensure that all system administrators use MFA even when SSO is enabled. SSO control is an important feature used to protect access to SaaS applications. However, some users intentionally circumvent SSO control. In situations such as maintenance sessions, SaaS vendors allow system owners to log in using their username and password even when SSO is enabled. Multi-factor authentication must be enabled for all superusers. Remember that if administrators use the same usernames and passwords, attackers will gain access to all accounts if an administrator's credentials are compromised.

- Fix shared mailboxes that are easy targets for hackers. A major challenge for many companies is the use of shared mailboxes for financial and customer data and other sensitive information. It is not uncommon to find an organization with one shared mailbox for every 20 employees. The problems that arise with shared mailboxes is that they have no clear owner and each user has a static password that does not change. These two problems are so serious that Microsoft even recommends blocking access to shared mailbox accounts.

- Use internal information access control to manage external users. Many companies use collaboration tools to exchange information. External sharing has many advantages, as it helps companies promote and extend their business to suppliers and partners. However, external sharing carries the risk of losing control over data. Put a collaboration policy in place to govern information sharing with external users and ensure that there are defined limits for all SaaS applications.

- Enable auditing to maximize control and visibility. Without question, you don't know what you don't see. Security teams need to stay on top of issues or information that you miss. The default auditing actions made available with SaaS apps are sufficient for some organizations. Some organizations will need more auditing options so they do not have to deal with security issues. Companies need to understand what they are not seeing and try to optimize security gaps.

- Tie up loose ends to ensure no data subsets are anonymously accessible. No data within the company should be accessible without the company's knowledge. Maintaining complete control over corporate data is not an easy task. The increasing use of SaaS applications will make it more difficult to maintain control of corporate data. You need to start by identifying all publicly exposed resources, including forms, discussions, dashboards, and any other data entities. Take immediate action to close the gaps and prevent data breaches and to put measures in place to ensure complete control of the data.

3

BLOCKCHAIN, AI & CYBERSECURITY

CHAPTER THREE

CYBERSECURITY AWARENESS

Security awareness has become an absolute trend for all those companies that have decided to turn their fortunes around by investing in hands-on security awareness training, which can help reduce the risk of breaches by about 70%. Infact, the whole group of technology tools, such as antivirus software, DNS-based security software, DLP, network intrusion systems, and web gateways, are not 100 percent effective in protecting networks and systems. These technological tools are essential and meet the requirements of best practices, but it is the human element that must be considered in protecting networks. Failure to protect the human element, which remains the main vulnerability, will lead to the total collapse of all other defenses. More than 90 percent of data breaches are caused by human error.

3.1. THE BUSINESS APPROACH TO CYBERSECURITY AWARENESS

In general, implementing an effective information security strategy requires a human-centered approach. One click on a button or a phishing email can allow a malicious actor to access the network and millions of files. A study revealed that 44 percent of errors caused by employees are due to lack of awareness of cybersecurity principles. Cybersecurity awareness should become part of an organization's culture to help it become more effective in protecting its assets. If training is offered frequently and timely, it will promote positive behavior change and reduce risk.

For an effective cybersecurity awareness culture, the following considerations must be carefully followed:

- Identify a team of champions from the different sectors/departments of the company to support security training programs. These champions will help engage the rest of the staff, even in departments that are not involved in cybersecurity.

- Ensure that the security team is able to respond immediately to any risky behavior exhibited by an employee on the network. Immediate corrective action will help the employee understand what the wrong/unacceptable behavior is at the time it occurs and help them reconsider their efforts the next time they encounter a similar situation. This type of training has a greater impact than routine activities that do not involve simulations of risky behavior.

- Reinforce continuous learning through formal training opportunities for employees who need assistance. Generalized training for all employees does not achieve the desired results throughout the company. Training should be based on IT knowledge assessment and other security simulations to ensure that learning outcomes are achieved and that all employees are aware of IT security policies and measures.

- Undertake quarterly simulations, especially regarding phishing attacks, to help employees understand what a real attack looks like and what to do when receiving such a message to avoid putting the organization at risk.

- Help employees understand that downloading software and applications from unverified sources or third-party sites is risky behavior that is contrary to company policy.

- Make all staff understand the importance of not saving data on file-sharing applications in the cloud and reinforce the message when risky behavior occurs through immediate training. - Explain why access to and use of TOR networks is not allowed to prevent the organization from being at risk of attacks.

- When hiring new staff, an organization should provide essential training and education to get them into the cybersecurity culture and help them prevent risky behavior in the future. This helps save the time and effort required to organize in-person sessions.
The organization must take a holistic approach to cybersecurity, starting with creating a "cybersecurity awareness culture" to reinforce behavioral awareness through education and training. Cybersecurity is not just the installation of flashy security tools. The holistic approach combines people, processes and technology to prevent attacks and data breaches.

3.2. CYBERSECURITY CHALLENGE WITH SMART WORKING

The COVID-19 pandemic has pushed organizations to work remotely. IT professionals believe the future of work will be fully remote or semi-remote (hybrid). According to numerous surveys, the average employee prefers to work from home a few days a week.
As a result of the shift to remote work, cyber security cases have increased dramatically, with organizations scrambling to get organized in time, exposing themselves more to cybercrime. Remote work has put continuous pressure on IT teams. The increase in cybersecurity incidents has been both in frequency and sophistication. A report

by Netscout indicates a 15 percent increase in Distributed Denial of Service (DDoS) attacks in the first half of 2020 compared to the similar period last year.

Working from home poses challenges and risks for companies without robust cybersecurity systems in place. Notable spikes in threats include gaps in end-point security and e-mail-based threats. Potential threats or points of attack when working remotely include:

- Unsecured home Wi-Fi network. Using weaker protocols on an employee's home Wi-Fi makes it easier for hackers to access network traffic. Other employees may access unprotected public Wi-Fi networks, which poses the risk of traffic interception and loss of confidential data.

- Phishing attacks and scams targeting remote workers. Employees are prone to click on malicious links and attachments contained in seemingly legitimate but misleading e-mails. Phishing attacks are one cause of data breaches.

- Weak passwords. Simple and insecure passwords make it easy for hackers to access networks and data. If a worker uses a similar password in all areas, attackers gain unauthorized access to multiple platforms with potential data loss.

- Vulnerability of technologies. The use of new and inadequately tested technologies poses unique cyber risks. Vulnerabilities in new technologies for remote work are potential weaknesses that can be exploited by malware. In addition, the involvement of third parties, such as IT service providers, increases cyber risks in the work environment.

- Use of personal devices. With employees working from home, many will use their own devices to complete assigned tasks. Potential security issues include the lack of custom firewalls, automatic backup tools, and robust antivirus software usually built into corporate networks. The risk of malware infection and data loss increases exponentially with the use of personal devices.

Organizations need to understand new cybersecurity challenges and revamp their strategies to address them. An organization's cybersecurity risk profile needs thorough assessments and monitoring to manage and mitigate threats.

Below, there are key points to build on when revamping your cybersecurity strategy, with reference to smart working as well:

1. Business and IT security personnel must work together to evaluate cybersecurity budgets and prioritize risk management and building

resilience.

2. Strategy on the use of unsecured access points. Remote work pushes employees outside the boundaries of the corporate network and access points. The danger of an unsecured access point becomes a greater risk. Employees must be instructed to be diligent when using devices from home and accessing Wi-Fi, especially in public spaces.
3. Simplify administrator rights and employee credentials. Review guidelines and requirements on how employees access data and communicate. Access restrictions, improved employee discipline, and robust data loss controls will reduce the risks associated with accessing and sharing private information.

4. Make changes that improve the technology and security infrastructure. Some transitional measures are regularly updating software with the latest security patches. Long-term measures may include migrating to more robust systems.

5. Create mechanisms to improve agility in responding to and addressing changes in security programs. Cybersecurity risks are a moving target with many emerging challenges that require special measures in response.

6. Enhance cyber awareness and training exercises to monitor and improve the cyber risk culture of employees, management teams, and IT teams. Remote work introduces new cyber threats that employees need to be aware of and prevent. Training and role-based exercises will help raise awareness, entrench rules and roles, and report cybersecurity incidents.

7. Set up a structured data backup strategy. All sensitive data should be encrypted to limit access to unauthorized persons. Try to diversify data backup, not relying on a single on-premises backup. The general rule of 3-2-1 is to have three different backups for sensitive information, two other backup formats, and an off-site backup in case of physical damage to the office or business premises.

3.3. FROM CYBERSECURITY AWARENESS TO EMPLOYEE BEHAVIOR CHANGE

Humans have been identified as the weakest link in the cybersecurity chain. Employees make mistakes because of inherent human characteristics such as malice, envy, defiance, and carelessness. Some of these mistakes can have catastrophic consequences for the organization's sensitive data and network infrastructure.

With the pressures of work and the many unfinished tasks, convincing employees to take the organization's security seriously is no easy task. Behavior change requires training and commitment that few employees are willing to make. Not surprisingly, no one cares. Just think of trying to convince employees in other departments to prioritize cybersecurity tasks that they do not see as their responsibility. Moreover, existing security awareness training programs are sporadic, irrelevant, and simply lack interest, negating the seriousness that should have been achieved.

Improving information security in an organization requires more than just awareness raising to effectively change employee security behavior. An effective behavior change program requires an audit of existing practices. Problem areas will be identified and used to inform the process design.

In practice, simply raising awareness of information security will not be the answer, nor will it support behavior change. This means that organizations must design and develop robust, human-centered security programs to address and reduce the number of incidences associated with employee security misconduct. The goal is to positively influence employee behavior to avoid playing catch-up or always reacting to incidents.

These are the critical elements that security teams must examine before influencing behavior:

- Seek to understand the critical factors that influence employee security choices;
- Design and deliver impactful security education, security awareness training, and general security awareness;
- Design and develop systems, applications, processes and physical environments that help account for user behavior;
- Develop metrics that help measure behavior change and show return on investment (ROI). The goal is for security to remain at the forefront of every employee's mind in order to promote more attentive and accurate behavior. The creation of human-centered security awareness programs will prove to be the tipping point for

ensuring top-notch security for the organization's networks and data. A good security education program acts as a deterrent, but it must be continuous to be effective.

The ultimate goal of security education and awareness is to empower users to make the right decisions by regularly reminding them of the guidelines on acceptable use of information systems and the potential outcomes if users do not follow the guidelines provided.

The ideal information security training program should follow the concept of microlearning. If you want to succeed in changing the organization's behavior, you must provide frequent, brief, and focused training to employees. Microlearning will not be effective in supporting behavior change if the content is not useful. Program content must be relevant, impactful and timely.

The benefits of these short but frequent trainings are to eliminate opportunities to forget or ignore something about information security. Also, it is important not to overwhelm employees with too much knowledge for one session. Achieving balance means having won a significant part of the battle to get all employees on board and protect the organization's data and network. Getting all employees thinking about information security will help eliminate or dramatically reduce the most obvious errors.

3.4. CYBERSECURITY: THE PEOPLE-CENTRIC STRATEGY

Organizations, or companies, have embraced technology and connectivity in all its aspects. Companies operating in remote and distributed work environments outsource functions to third-party partners and invest in cloud and SaaS applications. The adoption of different technologies, applications, or devices and working remotely represent an additional attack surface/opportunity that introduces new complexities into the cybersecurity equation. In fact, as we have seen, it is not only companies that are embracing the digital space, but cybercriminals as well. This is why companies need to strike a balance between keeping up with technological innovations and being truly successful.

In practice, cybersecurity can no longer be a "check box" issue; rather, organizations can leverage cybersecurity as a strategic tool to achieve business goals and build customer trust. Cybersecurity strategy is evolving from being technology-centric to being people-centric.

Cybersecurity should not only be viewed from the perspective of threats and their management. Cybersecurity is a strategic business driver, which implies that companies need to ensure organization-wide transformation efforts to consider cybersecurity proactively. Business leaders must actively participate in cybersecurity discussions. A 2022 PwC survey, which asked senior leaders how they frame the cyber mission in their organization, indicates that 54 percent of CEOs chose to focus on the big picture and growth objectives of their cyber security teams. Twenty percent of respondents believe that the first mission of cyber teams is to build trust with customers regarding the protection of their data and the ethical use of collected data.

Companies can maximize their value through cybersecurity in two ways:

1) Creating a cybersecurity culture in the organization that ensures effective collaboration between business development, technology and cybersecurity teams. In this way, cybersecurity is positioned as one of the critical pillars of any organization's value system. The process starts at the top: the board of directors must mandate senior leadership to drive cybersecurity outcomes. Board members must be encouraged to participate in tabletop exercises to remain aware of their roles and responsibilities in responding to cybersecurity threats. Business leaders need to set the right example for their teams and be vocal. Regular updates to the cybersecurity plan help the board move from compliance-based prioritization to risk-based prioritization, decision-making, and communication. An effective top management response will ensure support for funding decisions, prioritization of initiatives, and the necessary executive attention.

The goal is to build a culture that empowers cybersecurity teams to serve as a conduit for technical assistance in implementing cybersecurity requirements and to solicit feedback from lines of business to improve cybersecurity strategy. In addition, cybersecurity teams are able to interact productively with technology, marketing, and product teams to support large-scale digital transformation initiatives. For example, companies can address infrastructure and resource constraints by making all employees an extended arm of the cybersecurity team. A strong cybersecurity culture also requires that security team leaders actively collaborate with peer organizations, security user groups, and intelligence feeds that help companies stay current with the evolving cybersecurity landscape. Through ongoing role-based training, security professionals must maintain a high level of competence.

2) Effective communication of the impact of an organization's cybersecurity capabilities on customer satisfaction. Leaders of cybersecurity teams must define and publish cyber risk mission and vision statements that align with the organization's purpose, values, and goals. These statements should embrace the identity of the organization and communicate the approach to cyber risk management to customers. Likewise, they help align future program initiatives to measure and assess impact.

Ensure that customers receive information about the organization's capabilities to monitor cyber threats, analysis of long-term cybersecurity impact, and integration of cybersecurity considerations into customer offerings. Companies need to create transparent lines of communication with customers.

Companies have moved online and need to offer customers visibility into their data security capabilities to promote greater confidence in managing their data.

In conclusion, cybersecurity affects all aspects of life and is never a purely technical business issue. Organizations need to stop viewing cybersecurity as an abstract, cumbersome and intangible topic. Throwing money at the problem does not offer long-term solutions. A good cybersecurity strategy requires proactive collaboration, a "we're in this together" approach that links the goals of IT security teams and executive leadership. Effective cybersecurity programs and increased security awareness will protect corporate assets and information and prevent the consequences of breaches. Customers are key stakeholders in a successful, future-oriented organization.

4
BLOCKCHAIN,
AI & CYBERSECURITY

CHAPTER FOUR

CYBERCRIME AGAINST COMPANIES AND GOVERNMENTS

4.1. CYBERCRIME AND BUSINESSES (ESPECIALLY SMALL AND MEDIUM BUSINESS)

Cyberattacks can get everyone. Cybersecurity incidents are on the rise, and no company is completely safe from being blocked by hackers. Cybercriminals can especially target large companies and multinational enterprises, but smaller businesses are also a major target. A common but inaccurate belief among many small and medium-sized businesses (SMBs) is that the most excellent security vulnerabilities are found in large companies.

Cybercriminals target companies of all sizes and with devastating impact. Small and medium-sized businesses are usually hit in a variety of ways, including malware attacks. The motive is to steal customer data and information, damage reputation, and sabotage the company. Some small businesses are targeted for attacks and serve as a conduit to target large businesses that are their customers.

A common misconception is that small and medium-sized businesses are not as prone to cyber attacks as large companies. Another misconception is that SMBs do not need the same level of security. These misconceptions, complacency, and weak or nonexistent cybersecurity measures make SMBs a prime target for cybercriminals. Criminals use technology to launch quick and effective attacks and to gain even a small financial reward. Company size, length of time in business or industry do not matter. SMBs, regardless of industry, cannot afford to take a wait-and-see approach to cybersecurity. The realization that cyber threats are imminent always comes when it is too late for small businesses. Most SMBs may not survive a cyber-attack, and if they do, it may take several years to recover and repair the reputational damage. Sixty percent of small businesses that suffer a cyber-attack fail to recover and collapse. Failure to take sufficient cybersecurity measures will make the business an easy target for cyber attacks.

The same reasons why cybercriminals target large, successful companies also apply to SMBs. Any successful company today focuses on revenue growth. It increasingly relies on the Internet to carry out daily activities and store sensitive data, which makes it attractive to criminal enterprises. The global cyber criminal enterprise is estimated to have reached $1.5 trillion and growing.

SMBs may lack adequate funds and human resources to implement robust cybersecurity measures. In addition, SMBs are a very important target and are subject to repeated incidents of spyware, hacker intrusions, malware, ransomware, spam, and viruses. Any cybersecurity incident can cause downtime, loss of sales, loss of data, impact on production, and damage to reputation. Cybercriminals find a path of least resistance: they do not have to deal with the layers of complex security systems implemented by large companies.

SMBs need similar levels of protection as large companies. Security systems do not have to be as expensive or complicated as those adopted by large companies. However, SMBs need a robust and comprehensive security solution that meets their cybersecurity needs. Managed service providers (MSPs) offer all-in-one security solutions for SMBs and monitoring and training programs to meet their cybersecurity needs.

The most common ways in which hackers can target SMBs are:

- Social Engineering: Hackers exploit human nature to get people to download malware or provide their own login information to malware or to provide their login information to steal data or access a network.

- Watering hole attacks: Hackers try to use another company's services to gain access to a larger company through sites not a larger company through unprotected sites.

- Damaging business reputation: A data breach can irreparably damage the importance of the small businesses. It only takes a few seconds or minutes for a hacker to destroy many years of hard work.

- Financial loss: a security breach can put a company out of business, especially if finances are at stake. Security breaches are also difficult to deal with.

Well, then how can SMBs protect themselves? SMBs need to be proactive in preventing cyber attacks. It is less expensive and more convenient to prevent attacks than to recover from them, for both large and small businesses. Some steps SMBs can take to protect their network and business data are:

- Install a next-generation firewall - A firewall is the network's first line of defense. Firewalls ensure the security of traffic by inspecting the data passing through the system.

- Use updated antivirus software - All users should have up-to-date software antivirus installed to protect files, documents, PCs and block network intrusions.

- Have social media use policies - Cybercriminals use social media to gather information and enhance their attacks. Employees should be trained on how to share information on social media, including on their own pages.

- Filter email spam - Spam filtering helps prevent suspicious emails from arriving in inboxes. SMBs will need to fend off phishing and

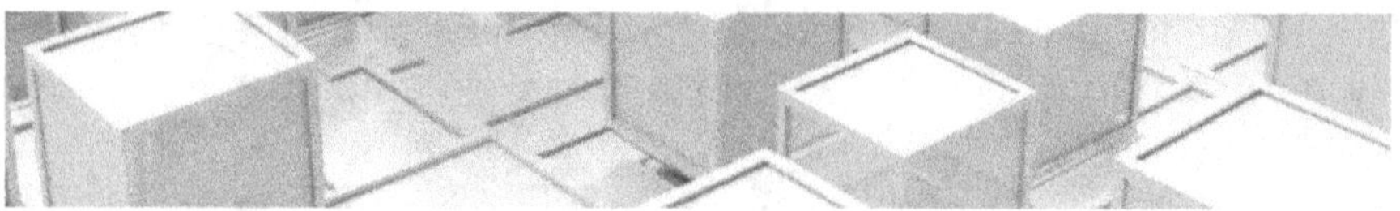

malware attacks.

SSL inspection-Make sure you can inspect SSL traffic to prevent threats and track data that employees send outside the company.

Another factor to consider for cyber attacks is time. The holidays, for example, give attackers the opportunity to plan and execute a successful compromise. Security researchers have recorded a 30% increase in the number of attempted ransomware attacks worldwide during the holiday season in consecutive years from 2018 to 2020.

This happens because companies are less prepared to fend off a cyber attack as employees have left for the vacations. In addition, employees and other end users rarely think about cybersecurity when they open emails and surf the web looking for vacation deals. Most people let their guard down in one way or another, distracting themselves from the prospect of enjoying the vacations. A distracted end user and mindlessly opening emails in search of vacation discounts and deals will provide attackers with opportunities to set up phishing scams and malicious advertisements. Short-staffed companies, as cybersecurity and IT professionals retire for the vacations, are at greater risk. There are fewer resources to address potential challenges, risks and breaches when they occur.

The Cybersecurity & Infrastructure Security Agency and the FBI recently issued a general warning for companies to increase vigilance against ransomware attacks during the vacations. The following are the most common cybersecurity risks during the holidays: - Ransomware. It is the main threat to businesses and their data during the holiday season. The risk of visiting malicious websites and experiencing phishing attacks increases exponentially, posing a significant threat to businesses. Ransomware is mistakenly described as an encryption problem. However, this misunderstanding undermines the determination and creativity of attackers in breaking into networks and crawling within an organization's digital environment to discover, steal and encrypt data. Ransomware can be very costly for companies. On average, ransomware attacks cost companies $4.62 million, including the costs of notification, escalation, loss of business, and response. The cost does not include the amount of ransom demanded.

Attackers induce users to click on malicious links contained in phishing emails or perform a drive-by attack using malicious web code on a hijacked website. These two methods serve as a gateway for ransomware infection. Notable ransomware attacks that occurred over the holidays include the Memorial Day attack on JBS, the meat processing giant, and the July 4 attack on Kaseya, an IT management software company. Companies can take some measures to protect themselves from ransomware, including putting in place: application whitelisting, access with minimal privileges, micro-segmentation, strong password policies and protection of hacked passwords and phishing email filtering.

- Phishing emails. They are an easy way for attackers to compromise networks. A phishing email looks like a communication from legitimate companies. Cybercriminals have become adept at making phishing emails look like legitimate emails by including logos, text, images, and styles. Without adequate security protections, end users will click on malicious links, setting widespread damage in motion. With no boundaries of zero trust and micro-segmentation, ransomware crawls freely within the network and infects everything a user account has permissions to. During the holiday season, end users are greedy for clicks and never take the time to carefully check email communications. Attackers are aware of this fact and send out a barrage of e-mails in an attempt to infiltrate an organization's network with a phishing attack.

The basics of cybersecurity-filtering phishing emails, disallowed attachments, and end-user cybersecurity training-will protect against phishing attacks.

- Data breaches. They are another major challenge for organizations around the world. The implications of a data breach can be far-reaching both in terms of impact and financial loss. The costs of data breaches increased from $3.86 million in 2020 to $4.24 million in 2021. Data breaches often occur as a result of malicious cyber attacks, both intentional and unintentional. Employees may deliberately or accidentally share data with unauthorized persons. Employees are typically distracted during the holiday season and may expose critical data.

- Distributed Denial of Service (DDoS) attacks. The holidays are also an opportune time to launch distributed denial of service (DDoS) attacks. DDoS attacks have been found to increase during the holidays. Online shopping is a big deal during the holidays and is a time when attackers launch DDoS attacks that are costly to businesses. Organizations need to adopt network mitigation and server technologies that protect against DDoS attacks.

- Breached passwords. Cybercriminals are finding ways to compromise environments using stolen or compromised credentials. It is easier to obtain compromised credentials and do considerable damage to business-critical data with minimal effort. It repeats the same theme of distracted employees during the vacations, who become easier targets. Ransomware attacks are launched to harvest legitimate credentials and verified user accounts. Attackers also choose to purchase user credentials on the dark web to eliminate the hard work of logging in. Compromised credentials are the most commonly used initial attack vector and account for 20% of data breaches. Breached passwords are the most costly cause of data breaches and have longer life cycles than other types of data breaches. Organizations need to strengthen password policies and implement adequate protection for breached passwords.

Organizations need to strengthen cybersecurity strategies and posture during the holiday season to prevent the listed challenges.

4.2. CYBERCRIME AGAINST GOVERNMENTS: PRIVACY AND SECURITY

Cybersecurity is a greater concern for governments than for individual users of cyberspace. Threats to the government may not raise the same level of alarm for the public, who may see them as minor inconveniences. The promulgation of Internet regulations to address cybersecurity is met with strong resistance from several sectors. The general feeling is that the legislation fundamentally affects Internet users and violates their privacy. People prefer to live with the inconvenience caused by cybercrime while maintaining their privacy and anonymity on the Internet.

Intelligence and law enforcement agencies have sought to expand mandates to investigate and prosecute Internet crimes. One reason given is that advances in computer networks and digital communication have complicated law enforcement. For example, encryption is no longer the preserve of the government and corporations. Criminals are also encrypting their documents and communications. Legislation to address existing and emerging loopholes has raised privacy concerns and resistance to an expanding big brother role for government. The difficult question is how to balance the government's need to protect critical infrastructure and sovereignty with personal privacy needs. Technology is advancing rapidly, and it is difficult to see how it will affect our lives. The need to protect critical information systems that support the economy and national defense from shutdown and infiltration is a major concern.

The debate has just begun and pits privacy advocates against the government. The drafting of any cybersecurity law must be guided by principles.

First, technology has changed individual privacy in fundamental ways. Private information is in the form of electronic files on computers or networks. Communications have also shifted to more diverse electronic means, and personal information is in the hands of unidentifiable third parties. Second, all laws must adapt to technological changes and the effect these have had on privacy protection. A war of attrition may ensue, as law enforcement agencies will want to maintain and expand surveillance capabilities while the public seeks to protect itself from the intrusion of its privacy. Third, critical infrastructure protection should be voluntary and organized by the private sector, rather than mandated by the government. Risky networks and infrastructure are managed and maintained by the companies that own them. Private sector-led solutions will work better for affected industries.

Cybersecurity and privacy protection will be the subject of a lengthy negotiation through new legislation. It is a give-and-take situation: gains in privacy protection must be jealously guarded, even if some level of privacy can be given up to deal with emerging cyber threats.

4.3. THE GOVERNMENT'S COMPLEX CHALLENGE: HACKERS AND TERRORISTS

Cyberthreats, network security, and sensitive information pose complex challenges to governments, especially with regard to national security and public policy. Cyber-based threats are proving to be the most significant threat to national security in many countries around the world. Unfortunately, the widespread adoption of technology has proven to be a double-edged sword: technology has been exploited by organized criminal groups and associations, terrorists, and even state-sponsored hackers to hijack critical infrastructure in support of commerce, national economies, military installations, and public safety.

Hackers and other actors focus on stealing state secrets, trade secrets, latest technologies and essential data, personal data, and any other valuable critical items. Terrorists and state-sponsored actors target critical infrastructure and installations, various sectors of the economy, propaganda promotion tools, and free speech. It is no longer possible to physically invade nation-states, and adversaries have decided to launch destructive cyber attacks. A well-coordinated cyber attack could be more devastating, in terms of lives and the economy, than the consequences of 9/11 in the United States. The consequences of power outages, flight cancellations, and communication disruptions caused by natural phenomena can be

used to assess the effects of cyber-attacks and cyber-terrorism.
The most serious threat to governments is high-level network intrusions perpetrated by state-sponsored actors and global criminal organizations that aim to compromise national security, the economy and public safety. Critical infrastructure relies heavily on computer networks, and in some cases, redundancy has not been built into these systems. This means that a network intrusion can cause devastating damage to human life and an entire economy. In recent years, the frequency and severity of cyber attacks on government infrastructure and the private sector have increased significantly. Companies have had to deal with network intrusions and data breaches and ransom demands to regain control of critical data and networks. Studies reveal that malicious botnets used by cybercriminals have cost companies billions of dollars in damages in recent years. In addition, the shift to working remotely, necessitated by the COVID-19 pandemic, has caused intrusions and data breaches to increase dramatically in the past year across all sectors.
Cyber attacks are becoming increasingly sophisticated, and criminals and adversaries are seeking to destroy critical infrastructure with cyber controls, such as banks, energy facilities such as dams and power grids, and transportation systems. In addition, factors such as the ease with which malware can be spread have enabled hackers and other actors to exploit millions of compromised servers, computers, and other network-connected devices to disrupt business and government operations.
Governments face the challenge of stopping cyber threats and attacks. Most cyber infrastructure is in the private sector, including power generation, banking, communications, and all other sectors of the economy. However, coordinated efforts against cyber threats are still a distant goal, as private sector companies avoid disclosing

attacks and sharing information for fear of lawsuits and upsetting shareholders.

Despite numerous cybersecurity products that promise quick fixes, the sophistication and persistence of attacks require the development and deployment of equally sophisticated solutions. This has forced states to institute measures to curb cyber threats through technical capabilities, electronic surveillance, forensic analysis and even physical surveillance. A report by the U.S. Cyber Command indicates that a day is coming when attacks on network infrastructures will turn to theft destruction and joint disruption. In addition to increasing in scope and scale, cyber threats are becoming more challenging to technical capabilities and investigative resources. Cybercriminals are devising ingenious and sophisticated ways to facilitate their nefarious activities. Challenges include lowering barriers to entry as cybercriminals aggregate and share tools on online forums, obfuscating identities, and renting and compromising infrastructure to hide malicious activities.

Faced with the increasing sophistication of attacks, governments are now focused on coordinating with partners around the world and are exploring various initiatives to stem the onslaught of cyber threats. The main focus is on improving threat identification and developing information-sharing mechanisms both within government and the private sector. States are also exploring and promoting partnerships in the fight against cybercrime and cyberterrorism. In addition, efforts are being made to coordinate with public and private partners to address the various challenges of cybercrime and cyberterrorism.

In addition, governments are investing in developing and retaining talent to address the challenges associated with cyber threats. The shortage of network security experts is a significant problem in combating cyber threats both within government and the private sector. We are not developing skilled professionals fast enough to fill existing gaps and address the technical capabilities of sophisticated attacks. As a result, programs have been established in schools to generate interest in cybersecurity and cultivate identified talent. In addition, the government is collaborating with academic institutions to study cybersecurity trends and develop solutions to stop these threats.

Lastly, cybersecurity should be integrated into technology solutions used in both the public and private sectors. Government and industry should work on legislation and policies governing the implementation of technology solutions so that cybersecurity is at the center from the beginning. Integrating cybersecurity into solutions will help reduce costs and improve resilience in the face of cyber attacks. Again, this is about considering cyber in everything the government and private

sector does.

In conclusion, governments must respond appropriately through policy and information sharing to increase interdependence across economies and global value chains. The goal should be to emphasize cooperation among nations to fight cyber threats.

5

BLOCKCHAIN, AI & CYBERSECURITY

CHAPTER FIVE

CYBERSECURITY: THE CURRENT SITUATION

The cybersecurity landscape will be dotted with new challenges and evolving threats. In addition, there will be new cybersecurity tools and technologies that can help improve defenses.

5.1. RECENT TRENDS IN ATTACK METHODOLOGIES

The task of predicting the future with a significant degree of specificity is not easy. In most cases, IT professionals can only make vague predictions that can be interpreted as inference. The cybersecurity landscape can be analyzed through recent trends in attack methodologies, emerging changes and new technologies, and the proliferation of threat actors. All of these factors help predict how the situation will evolve in the future.

Here, there are some predictions for cybersecurity:

- Evolution of Ransomware. We have seen the rise and fall of several trends in the cybersecurity space. Ransomware has been a big issue as of 2020. Attackers will try to steal data and encrypt it as an extortion tactic.

Ransomware will become a major concern for the healthcare industry as attacks seek to steal patients' medical records and extort them by threatening to make their medical histories public. It is feared that persistent attacks on medical infrastructure and medical records could lead to tragic outcomes. The healthcare sector needs to strengthen its defenses to keep malicious attackers at bay. Cybercriminals are expected to become bolder in their nefarious plans and target a wide range of sectors. We will see more targeted attacks against businesses and companies that were not previously considered high-risk.

- Automated Spear Phishing Attacks. The COVID-19 pandemic has been associated with an increase in automated spear-phishing attacks. The impact of the pandemic will continue through 2021 as economies collapse and fears increase.

We will see the use of automated tools by cybercriminals seeking to steal credentials and other private data from unsuspecting Internet users. However, automation will also benefit businesses by making it easier and reducing malicious activities.

- Zero-day attacks. We should see a significant increase in zero-day attacks against popular operating systems. Applications will not be spared, as attackers will try to take advantage of their spread. Developers will have to do their homework and be careful when putting software and applications into circulation. One way to address the challenge is through bug bounties offered by major vendors so that people will help identify bugs and improve their code. Cybercriminals have been using the same version of software and offering even higher payments to those who remember and sell them exploits.

- Targeting of remote workforce. More and more companies are adopting VPN and Remote Desktop Protocol (RDP) solutions to protect and support remote work. These solutions are used to connect remote connections used by employees working from home. In 2020, there has been a sharp increase in the remote workforce due to the pandemic. According to projections, the world will slowly move toward the remote work solution. By 2021, more work will be organized and completed remotely.
As a result, attacks targeting VPNs and RPP solutions will increase exponentially in 2021. Cybercriminals will seek to exploit and compromise remote connection servers and VPNs in order to gain direct access to corporate networks.

- Cryptocurrencies. Crypto has become the mode of payment for cybercriminals because of the privacy they offer. Government agencies blatantly despise cryptocurrencies and are working to regulate this sector. In 2021 we may see increased scrutiny and, in some cases, a ban on the use of cryptocurrencies. The driving force is to try to gain control over a growing cybercriminal underground. However, it will require cooperation from governments around the world. Another challenge with cryptocurrencies is crypto miners. Attacks use payloads that seek to gain control of computing resources. We can expect to see more cases in 2021.
- IoT technology. As more industries embrace the Internet of Things, we expect to see a concurrent increase in attacks targeting IoT devices, including connected cars. Attackers will target large devices, such as medical imaging systems, as well as smaller IoT devices that are unmatched and vulnerable. Malicious actors will find innovative ways to use compromised IoT devices. The priority will be to use IoT devices to compromise the cloud-based controllers on which the devices rely on.
One area of concern is autonomous driving technology, as more manufacturers adopt these systems and cybercriminals are finding ways to compromise the technology. Some of the attacks will be proof-of-concept, and will involve autonomous driving systems stopping in front of nonexistent obstacles or following road signs in unexpected places. There is a potential for serious attacks on the software and cloud infrastructure used for autonomous driving technology.
In conclusion, it is difficult to predict what will happen in the

cybersecurity industry in 2021. However, some of the trends that began in 2020 will continue and even explode in the new year. Other challenges that will arise from time to time are to target legacy endpoints as vendors withdraw support for some of their product offerings. Businesses that do not use multi-factor authentication may suffer an intrusion, and weak areas are targets for cybercriminals. Widespread adoption of MFA will help minimize the occurrence of data theft and phishing attacks. Companies need to stay one step ahead of malicious attackers. It is not easy, but the emergence of new tools and technologies can help improve defenses.

5.2. CYBER SKILLS GAP: THE WORKFORCE PROBLEM IN CYBERSECURITY

The global cybersecurity workforce gap has shrunk from 4 million to 3.1 million in 2020, marking the first time there has been a year-over-year reduction. According to data from the International Information System Security Certification Consortium - ICS, the gap has also narrowed in the United States, where the figure has dropped from 498,000 to 359,000 open jobs. There are about 880,000 active IT professionals. Overall, the cybersecurity skills situation continues to deteriorate over the past four years. The number of years it takes to acquire cybersecurity skills is also a cause of the cybersecurity skills gap. On average, it takes 3-5 years to achieve cybersecurity skills. The effects of the cybersecurity skills gap include increased workloads, the inability of organizations to effectively use cybersecurity tools, and the inability to fill open positions with the right skills. No significant progress has been made in addressing the supply and demand for cybersecurity professionals.

Despite the reported decline, the gap is still large and poses a significant threat to organizations in the face of increasing numbers of cyber attacks and incidents. Fifty-six percent of the 3,790 cybersecurity professionals surveyed globally acknowledged that staffing shortages could put their organizations at risk of attacks even if cyber incidents remain at baseline levels. Data from CyberSeek, an initiative that seeks to provide data to measure supply and demand in the cyber job market, indicate that the skills gap is actually widening rather than narrowing. A comparison reveals that in October 2019 there were 508,000 unfilled positions and 922,720 employed professionals, compared to 521,617 unfilled positions and 941,904 employed professionals in September 2020.

Cybersecurity professionals do not have a well-defined career path, and this is a contributing factor to the growing skills gap. Cybersecurity as a profession requires hands-on experience for those joining the industry, which in itself is a significant handicap. Qualifying for these jobs requires workers to have worked in cybersecurity to gain the necessary experience. New cybersecurity talent has a big mountain to climb before being successful in the industry.

The methodology adopted by ICS to arrive at the cybersecurity skills gap is different, in that the gap is described as the difference between the number of skilled professionals organizations need to protect their critical assets and the actual capacity available to do this work. Many industry groups agree with the conclusions reached by ICS that the skills gap poses a major security risk to organizations. CyberSeek adds that the shortage of cybersecurity professionals is approaching dangerous levels, with devastating effects on digital privacy and critical infrastructure. The ISC survey also revealed that 12 percent of respondents said the severe cyber manpower shortage put their organizations at extreme risk; 40 percent said their organizations were at moderate risk. Another 20 percent said their organization had a significant shortage of cybersecurity personnel. Another 40 percent, however, said they did not need cybersecurity professionals. The reduction in the skills gap in 2020 was attributed to a reduction in the average demand for personnel across segments, which led to a reduction in investment in hiring cybersecurity professionals. The global market for cybersecurity professionals decreased by about 5% compared to 2019. There has been a sharp decline in the total number of U.S. companies-including small and medium-sized businesses-that have hired and invested in cybersecurity professionals. Large companies have invested slightly more in cybersecurity professionals than in 2019, but levels are still relatively lower. Overall, the demand for personnel decreased by 5% compared to 2019 and was attributed to the impact of the COVID-19 pandemic on personnel budgets and businesses.

In addition, the estimated supply of available talent increased by 25% year-on-year. An estimated 3.5 million people work in cybersecurity. Cybersecurity positions take about 21% longer to fill than other IT jobs. According to the ISC, the increase, which translates to about 700,000 more professionals, is attributed to companies increasingly investing in their teams of cybersecurity professionals and the growth of the industry. Additional data reveal that cybersecurity employment needs to grow by about 89 percent globally and 41% in the United States to fill the current talent shortage. The talent shortage remains a major concern for cybersecurity professionals in the face of increasing cyber attacks and incidents.

The increase in the supply of cybersecurity professionals has been good news for the industry in recent years. It is hoped that it will become a turning point for an industry that had previously failed to attract new talent.

Organizations need to strategize and realign their cybersecurity needs to address them holistically. Some companies focus their investments only on technology, instead of investing in training and upgrading security professionals to better protect networks and data. The cybersecurity strategy must support the company/organization's strategy in goals such as revenue generation.

5.3. SMALL SAFETY TEAMS: FIVE IMPORTANT SECURITY LESSONS

Remote working presented its own challenges as bunesses scrambled to facilitate a seamless transition and faced massive cyber attack surfaces. Cybersecurity challenges have increased exponentially, and security teams have been strained as they attempt to respond and protect critical infrastructure and data.

Companies have slowly realized that it will no longer be possible to require all employees to go to the office every day. A digital transformation has taken place, and remote work is here to stay. How should companies prepare for the new dynamic of hybrid work? Their small security teams will need to review security strategies, planning and execution to address many day-to-day challenges. Below, there are practical tips and recommendations that will help small and medium-sized businesses prepare for the new reality:

1. Accept that you can't do it all: One practical way to virtually expand a small business's security team is to ask the security vendor about the services offered. You will be surprised to discover a wide range of complementary services provided alongside their paid offerings. This is an opportunity that many small businesses miss primarily by not asking for it, but it can be leveraged to effectively provide increased security for remote and in-house workers. 2. Response Speed is critical: Automation of security services is a step in the right direction for small and medium-sized business security teams. Indeed, speed of response to security incidents and challenges is the watchword. Rapid response has been proven to reduce the cost of a data breach. Numerous factors can influence the speed of response after a cyber attack, including the size and maturity of an organization, the presence and effectiveness of employee training

programs, total staff and processes, and the people and technology in use. Speed of response is to identify threats, apply corrections, and restore regular service. Automation helps to significantly reduce the number of threats and prevent unexpected ones. It reduces the number of resources, both financial and human, deployed to combat cyber threats. Cybersecurity is effectively improved when automation is coupled with the right tools to provide impregnable protection of corporate data and resources. Data must be analyzed to identify suspicious activity that may indicate the presence of a threat within the network. Automation makes it possible to operate with speed and take proactive measures to improve cybersecurity. As cyber-attackers have embraced automation to launch attacks at lightning speed, companies cannot remain stuck on manual interventions. Automation enables companies to react faster and stay one step ahead of threat actors. In addition to protection, automation helps prevent similar attacks in the future.

3. Best practices for the numerous corporate devices issued to employees: The new reality of a hybrid work system will mean that more and more enterprise devices will be provided to employees to facilitate remote work. The security team must consider creating and training employees on best practices related to securing and managing all of these devices. Best practices will also apply to the security team itself, as it too will be working remotely.

4. Increasing supply chain attacks: Think about it: the security of your suppliers is your security problem, given the intertwined nature of today's supply chains. Small business security teams must continue to work, even with limited budgets, to identify the threats currently present in their environment and how they can be addressed to avoid disrupting the systems coupled with it.

5. Threat economies and landscapes are changing rapidly: In particular, ransomware is growing at astronomical levels. Companies must always safeguard their data and critical infrastructure from breaches or attacks. The best way to protect a business is to institute cross-cutting measures, from training to implementing technologies that best protect data and other assets.

In conclusion, small security teams faced a wide range of challenges. The situation has been further exacerbated by the pandemic and the transition to remote work and other hybrid work environments. The above measures will help maintain operations despite security teams being fully staffed and operating with limited budgets and human resources.

5.4. A MUST-HAVE FOR EVERY COMPANY: CYBERSECURITY PLANS

You never know when disaster may strike. Cybersecurity incidents are not created equal, and some can cause total devastation. Instructions for immediate security and recovery vary depending on the nature and scope of the incident.

Cyberattacks are diverse and can take the form of brute force accounts, phishing attacks and ransomware that require different security protocols. To effectively deal with cyber attacks, companies must have robust and actionable security plans in place to ensure the recovery and security of data and infrastructure. Security and recovery plans must be outlined based on the specific nature of the cyber disaster.

Companies must create and implement a business cybersecurity plan. By definition, a cybersecurity plan is essentially a playbook that outlines the roles of all key players, emergency contacts, and the framework for responding to all types of cyber incidents. A cybersecurity plan must report information beyond business interruption from a cyber incident and consider all of the company's IT infrastructure. Not only that, a comprehensive cybersecurity plan transcends basic "stop, drop and roll" instructions. Companies must recognize that cybersecurity is a rapidly evolving field, and any cybersecurity plan to protect a business must remain agile.

Here, there is what a good corporate cybersecurity plan should include:

1. A business-specific cybersecurity plan.
From the outset, the plan should explore and address how your company interacts with technology on a daily basis. Address critical issues such as whether your company accepts online payment card transactions, whether the organization collects sensitive data from your customers, whether the organization collects health data from patients, and whether there are significant systems open to the Internet that manage daily business operations. The corporate cybersecurity plan must comply with all applicable regulations, define the organization's priorities, provide necessary information to insurance companies, and consider all other needs of the organization.

2. Room for updates

A good cybersecurity plan provides room for updates and the inclusion of the latest security information and strategies. A good plan is considered a living document that is constantly changing based on the latest threat information, new third-party vendors that need to be involved, and new cyber attacks that you may be a victim of.

The ideal cybersecurity plan will not be a short set of instructions. In the world of cybersecurity, plan for frequent updates as the landscape changes. Always have an expert on hand to consult and help you implement new actions.

3. Cover your bases

Keep in mind that to protect a home, you cannot install smoke detectors in only half the rooms. Likewise, you cannot cover only part of your technology infrastructure. It would be helpful if you covered all your bases, taking into consideration cloud storage providers, e-mail service providers, third-party providers, and SaaS products. The scope of the infrastructure depends on the nature of your organization, and you need to address all aspects of the cybersecurity plan.

Every organization needs a customized cybersecurity plan that covers all aspects of its particular infrastructure architecture. A good cybersecurity plan includes proper communication channels, emergency contacts, and a holistic incident response plan. Emergency contacts should not just be a list of references as in a phone book. Emergency contacts should essentially organize teammates and assign roles on what each person needs to do in response to a cyber incident. The idea is to keep everyone on board in all departments, including IT, security, human resources, risk management, legal, and corporate communications. Establish appropriate communication channels within your cybersecurity plan, outlining primary and secondary contacts to eliminate confusion that could arise in the event of an ongoing cyber attack. You can also use the services of security experts to alert you to attacks and generate incident response. Two-thirds of cybersecurity professionals report a shortage of personnel in their organizations. Without access to adequate security talent, leaders lack visibility into how the security environment and threats have changed. Once communication and contacts are in order, companies are ready to move on to the incident response plan. Here, there are the guidelines:

1. Contain. Containing a cyberattack should be the first step in the incident response plan. Cyberattacks such as ransomware rely on spreading to as many devices within the network as possible. The first priority should be to contain an attack immediately after it is

identified. Containment will involve disconnecting devices from the network and engaging employees, incident response companies, and cyber insurance resources.

2. Assess. The next step is to preserve what is possible. Try to learn how an attacker infiltrated your network, what actions they took after entering, and how the attack was distributed. The information gathered will form the basis for evidence and general intelligence about the threat and will help restore data that may have been manipulated. Where possible, preserve forensic evidence, especially in the form of logs. Some evidence may be obtained from Managed Service Providers (MSPs) and other third-party vendors who possess logs that touch their infrastructure. Collecting and sifting through logs can be time-consuming, but it is still essential for threat intelligence, vulnerability identification, and protection of other companies.

3. Communicate. Communicate with stakeholders according to requirements, taking care to provide relevant information that affects them. Start by communicating to employees and how they can perform their duties while responding to the incidence. Prepare them for what to expect in the coming days and how to better protect their accounts. Always notify the appropriate authorities of the breach if sensitive data such as SSNs and credit card numbers are stolen.

4. Learn. No cyber attack is similar to the previous one. However, there is always something new to learn from cyber vulnerabilities and incidents. Constantly learn and tailor your cybersecurity plan based on lessons learned from the previous incident and apply organization-wide changes as necessary.
Careful analysis and research will help prioritize areas of concern and design a strategy that can significantly mitigate the company's risk.
In conclusion, proper planning, regular updates, and the presence of trusted cybersecurity experts will help the company remain secure and agile in the face of cyberattacks.

6

BLOCKCHAIN, AI & CYBERSECURITY

CHAPTER SIX

CYBERSECURITY TYPES AND STRATEGIES

There are several application levels for security. In this section, some practical cybersecurity methods are listed.

6.1. PROTECT YOURSELF WITH ENCRYPTION TO PREVENT DATA BREACHES

Security challenges will not go away anytime soon as old technologies become obsolete and new ones emerge. Legacy systems will no longer be patchable and will become easy targets for cybercriminals who will always find ways to attack and exploit new technologies implemented by companies. In this scenario, organizations and businesses must seek to protect their data at all costs, regardless of where it is stored. No data is safe, whether it is stored in the cloud or on a server. The first step is to encrypt all data to make it secure. However, it is good to know that the encryption required is not enough to keep data safe. Disk-level encryption is used to protect the storage medium as

a whole from attack or unauthorized use. The entire disk is encrypted with a single encryption key stored in the same hardware or in disk-level encryption schemes on the same disk as the encrypted data. The advantage of this arrangement is that developers can easily change the encryption key when the need arises. However, it makes it easy for hackers to gain access to sensitive information. Up to 75% of data breaches begin with the theft of credentials from an account with privileges. Attackers steal user credentials to access the encryption key and gain access to information stored on the drive. Alternatively, attackers may choose to download the encryption key and encryption data and decrypt them at offline locations. Access to the credentials of a privileged account means that all apps linked to it can access the unencrypted data once logged in. Attackers will have found a large attack surface to access sensitive data.

It is discouraging to know that sensitive data can be leaked or stolen even when it is encrypted. The situation is due to the fact that many companies approach information security in a piecemeal manner, leaving gaps that are easily exploited by cybercriminals. Encryption must occur at all layers of the TCP/IP stack. Security teams must understand that when encrypting a specific point on the stack, all other layers above it will not be protected. For example, data within a disk may be encrypted, but it will be tested immediately during transport in the network layer. The security of networks and stored data must be at the forefront of all activities. Response measures do not sufficiently protect sensitive data and often arrive when it is already too late.

Another challenge is developers launching products directly to market as soon as they are completed, as quickly as possible. The high rate at which applications and software are released before they are tested by security teams means that users are exposed. There is no quality control and security testing, so some developers use broken algorithms, outdated encryption strategies, and distribute applications with bugs. Customers or users realize too late that products already distributed are susceptible to attacks.

The approach of building a ring around the network or hardware is not sufficient to prevent data breaches. All major data breaches in both the private and public sectors have occurred at the application level. This includes all versions of data breaches, including advanced persistent threat (APT) attacks and malware. To address these serious threats, data must be protected at the application layer. This means that the data must be encrypted by the application. Only the application will have access to the encryption key when it accesses the data. When FDE, TDE and TLS encryption are used alone, they are mostly insufficient to protect sensitive data. Additional measures include preventing individual users and third-party applications from accessing encrypted data or encryption keys. This will help reduce the organization's attack surface. The only way an attacker can access encrypted data is through application functionality. In this way, IT teams can verify access control issues and permissions.

Application-level data security requires organizations to engage developers and security teams to protect data and applications. Security must be a fundamental part, embedded in all software and application development work. Security teams can help guide developers in using tools and processes that show the creation of secure applications.

Some of the tools available are APIs that can help encrypt data at the application level. Through just a few lines of code, developers can help encrypt and protect data without having to become cryptography professionals. You can be assured that customer data is safe and you no longer have to worry about threats and data breaches.

6.2. CLOUD DATA SECURITY. FOUR BEST PRACTICES FOR BUSINESSES

Businesses around the world have become dependent on the cloud for a wide range of mission-critical workflows. Companies now depend entirely on the cloud platform for HR processes, payroll processing, CRM data, etc. Companies have entrusted confidential data to their cloud providers. Most companies adopt a "load and forget" approach, especially for sensitive business data. Adherence to cloud security best practices should ensure that data and business operations are protected.

Here, there are four best practices that companies should lead:

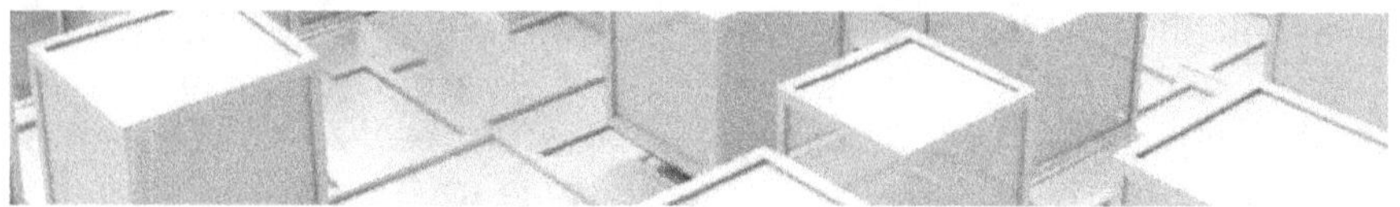

1. Conducting due diligence

When choosing a cloud vendor/vendor, the first step is a thorough due diligence. The company should investigate each vendor to learn more about security practices, reputation, and details of user agreements.

The bare minimum is to determine how and where the cloud provider will store data. The user also needs to know details about how the provider works to prevent unauthorized users from accessing his or her data.

The due diligence process should also help you find out whether the cloud provider offers technical support and safeguards in the event of a data breach. Failure to obtain clear and satisfactory information in any of the areas listed above should help you decide and choose a more reliable cloud provider.

2. Create a robust access management strategy

Create and implement an access management strategy that is unified and solid. The biggest challenge cloud-dependent companies face is dependence on fragmented authentication and access management systems. The effects are poor credential management and lack of explicit permissions.

Access management requires end-to-end lifecycle management of user identities and rights across all platforms and enterprise resources. It constitutes a fundamental control of cloud security, as it helps authenticate users and regulate access to cloud systems, networks, and data. The best way forward is to unify authentication and access management, preferably through a single sign-on (SSO) provider. The bare minimum is that all accounts require multi-factor authentication, regardless of platform. These accounts should also undergo frequent reviews of access rights to ensure sufficient data protection.

Finally, the strategy must also include measures to prevent identity theft. The growing number of identity theft cases means that companies must take proactive measures to ensure that the problem does not occur and data is compromised.

3. User education and malware protection

Company employees are the people entrusted with access to

essential data, and the ultimate responsibility for data security falls on them. Appropriate education and training on cloud security best practices must be provided. Without basic security training, all an employee needs is a spam email to facilitate a corporate data breach. Cloud security best practices should emphasize proper training of all users before accessing critical systems and workflows or corporate data. The movement should not stop there, but continue to remind users of their responsibilities, keep them on their toes, and inform them of emerging threats.

The other best practice for cloud security is to implement a malware protection solution specifically designed for cloud environments. Malware protection solutions offer features such as uploaded data scanning and proactive threat defense that prevent unauthorized users from accessing sensitive data hosted in the cloud. Malware protection solutions do not replace a base of well-trained, security-aware users, but they provide an excellent insurance policy that protects against inadvertent human error.

4. Data minimization

It may seem counterproductive to tell companies to minimize the data they upload to the cloud and actually entrust to cloud providers. However, reducing the data stored in the cloud will help reduce the risk of exposure and the need to institute comprehensive data protection measures. The precise idea is to refine business processes so that the data required to operate those processes or systems is as small as possible. A perfect example is managing a negotiation pipeline in the cloud, which usually involves storing personally identifiable customer data. For the system to be effective, it does not require complex financial data or more sensitive information beyond contact information. Data minimization means that companies can organize their system around customer contact information and ensure that all users avoid entering sensitive information that is not necessary for the system to function effectively. Companies will need to create data minimization policies that regulate the collection, storage, and use of data to reduce a company's vulnerability in the cloud. In some cases, the storage and use of specific types of data collected from customers are governed by regulatory requirements. The policy created must take regulatory requirements into account. Reducing the amount of data stored on different cloud platforms allows the company to simplify everything it needs to do to achieve data security. It simplifies data security, including data management, access control and retention processes. Data minimization should be at the heart of everything a company does online.

In conclusion, companies cannot give up on cloud platforms. Cloud platforms and cloud-based applications play a key role in the daily operations of businesses. The online threat environment is constantly evolving and becoming more challenging every day. Companies have a responsibility to ensure that the use of cloud platforms minimizes risk and promotes data security. Failure to establish and follow best practices for cloud data security is a fatal fate for a business. Having best practices and following them strictly will govern cloud use and ensure data security.

6.3. CYBERSECURITY: NOC VS SOC

Organizations seeking to protect and get the best out of their network should have a Network Operations Center (NOC), a Security Operations Center (SOC), or both. However, companies do not know how to distinguish between NOC and SOC and which team is best suited.

The Network Operations Center (NOC) is a team that is responsible for maintaining optimal network performance. It ensures that the enterprise network infrastructure adequately meets the needs of the business. Organizations use their network infrastructure for specific purposes, and the role of the NOC is to optimize and troubleshoot the network, ensuring that it meets the needs of the business.

A Network Operations Center forms the backbone of an organization's technology infrastructure. A dedicated NOC team provides 24/7 data protection for network performance, prevents downtime, and maintains uninterrupted service for critical applications, on-premise equipment, and cloud-based applications.

The team creates proactive workflows that ensure optimal enterprise network performance and uptime. Workflows include system monitoring, patching, and adherence to predetermined maintenance routines. Efficiently designed NOCs are based on the following: - 24/7 network, hardware and software health and optimization:

- Consistent data flow and data backup management - Network communications
- Proactive and constant monitoring
- Downtime reduction and alert management
- Remediation recommendations and roadmaps
- Reporting, including identification and analysis of trends
- Updates and patch management

The Security Operations Center (SOC) identifies, investigates, deters, and resolves cyberattacks and threats before they become problematic. The SOC team responds to threats in real time. It is responsible for protecting the network from cyber threats through

comprehensive, real-time, and cost-effective analysis of the network, endpoints, and cloud-based infrastructure. SOC teams include highly skilled cybersecurity specialists who are responsible for continuous threat monitoring, remediation, and analysis. In the enterprise environment, the SOC can be an internal team within the organization or provided by a third party under the SOC as a service model.
An agile SOC is engaged in:

- Real-time monitoring of network endpoint vulnerabilities 24/7
- Comprehensive investigations - understanding how and why a breach occurred and preventing future attacks.
- Research and analysis - examination of security log data, analysis of regular and irregular trends.
- Security policies and processes - to ensure compliance with the latest regulations.
- Threat detection and risk mitigation.
Both NOC and SOC are teams that have almost similar roles, but with significant differences that include:

1. Objectives - the main objective of the NOC and SOC is to ensure that the enterprise network meets the needs of the business. The main role of the NOC is to ensure that the network is able to meet service level agreements (SLAs) during normal operations and to deal with any natural disruptions, such as service interruptions and natural disasters. The main objective of the SOC is to protect the network and safeguard business operations from interference by cyber threat actors.

2. Adversaries - Although the NOC and SOC protect the corporate network from disruptions, they fight against different adversaries. The NOC will work to prevent network disruptions caused by natural causes such as natural disasters, power outages, and Internet outages. The SOC will protect the corporate network from man-made events such as different forms of cyber attacks.

3. Required Skillsets – NOC and SOC teams require similar skills to monitor a network and identify and resolve problems that cause outages and performance drops. The difference lies in the areas of focus and application of skills. NOC analysts use their skills to monitor and optimize network infrastructure and endpoints. SOC analysts have skills that are used to protect the enterprise network from human-driven threats and human actors. They must understand how

cyber attack chains work and have the skills to remediate infiltrations and malicious infections. The skills of SOC analysts are aimed at ensuring the security and resilience of enterprise IT assets.

The NOC vs. SOC Debate

Organizations should never be grappling with whether to create an NOC or SOC team. The ideal situation is to have both an NOC and a SOC. Organizations should clearly delineate the responsibilities of each team and ensure cohesive collaboration between the teams. Any potential crossover between the respective NOC and SOC coverage areas requires effective management.

Companies that need comprehensive network support, lack dedicated internal IT teams, and cannot afford network downtime should establish a network operations center.

An NOC will avoid huge downtime costs and productivity losses and, if necessary, help with network upgrades.

On the other hand, companies that need only security assistance will need the skills and experience of an SOC. The SOC team will monitor and mitigate cyber threats, keep records of network activity and communications, and ensure compliance with data privacy laws. Ultimately, the roles of NOC and SOC are complementary, as they focus on protecting the corporate network from potential risks that affect network performance and productivity. Despite differences in primary goals and tasks, NOC and SOC teams share the need for deep visibility and centralized control over the network infrastructure. Choosing only one team between NOC and SOC will make the organization vulnerable to natural or man-made events that cause network and business disruptions.

It is critical to have input from both the NOC and SOC to develop a comprehensive security plan. Without security plan integration, the organization risks security gaps, inconsistent processes, miscommunication, lack of transparency, and the use of outdated policies and tools, which cumulatively lead to increased threat/ vulnerability exposure.

6.4. MODERN SOC: 10 ESSENTIAL CAPABILITIES

An organization's cybersecurity strategy is implemented and coordinated by the Security Operation Center (SOC). The SOC manages security issues at both the technical and organizational levels. The main challenge for the cybersecurity industry is malicious actors using increasingly sophisticated tactics. There will never be enough qualified professionals to analyze and manage the volume of incidents that organizations face. Security teams are mired on the front lines of threat identification, analysis and mitigation.

The modern SOC must be powered by data and visibility across the organization, creating a common work surface for all team members. The SOC comprises three basic building blocks: people, processes and technology. The building blocks are linked together through governance and compliance frameworks.

Listed below, there are the essential capabilities of a modern SOC:

1. Ingest: All data in an organization is relevant. For the modern SOC, data is comparable to oxygen that gives and sustains life. Data drive analysis and algorithms and must be ingested from all sources and at scale. In addition, a SOC must be able to organize data and make it usable by humans and machines.

2. Detect: The SOC must be able to detect any event that enters the system. Detection must focus on possibilities rather than the files and network traffic expected by traditional solutions. The SOC must leverage correlation, analytics, and machine learning to detect events. Threat search and detection is a combination of human intuition and machine technology.

3. Predict: the SOC must predict an alert up to 30 minutes before discovering a security event. The ability to predict security events will help the SOC proactively report incidents to the right people/teams or organize a response using an already predefined process. Several emerging predictive technologies provide earlier warnings, precursors, and indicators of more significant attacks and can also identify unknowns before they become substantial risks.

4. Automate: SOC analysts must employ automation tools that use standard operating procedures to expedite investigation, threat detection, enrichment, containment, and remediation. Automation is one of the essential technologies available to SOC analysts. With

automation, an SOC can handle more events, as they typically take 30 minutes and can be executed in 40 seconds. Automation has become a mandatory tool.

5. Orchestrate: Typically, the modern SOC has the best or most expensive tools to power an organization's defense. However, the evolving nature of threats will make some tools obsolete in a short time. Products and tools must keep pace in an API-driven world and must be updated to keep up with the speed of evolving threats. Orchestration allows the SOC to connect everything inside and outside the SOC. You can use a single browser tab or unified logins for different products to eliminate copy and paste between solutions. With orchestration, you eliminate overhead and frustration buildup and focus on more critical activities.

6. Recommend: Imagine how great it would be if the platform that powers a SOC could tell analysts what steps to take. An event will have gone through several levels of the platform that powers the SOC to get to this point. A modern SOC will choose the best platform that can provide recommendations in digital playbooks or individual actions. Recommendation from the platform will have the following benefits: a) it is educational for new analysts who will know what to do if a similar threat arises; b) it is both a sanity test and an accelerator for analysts who are experts in what they already know.

7. Investigate: Investigations require detailed and precise human analysis. The use of intuitive security tools will help analysts prioritize the security needs that need to be investigated. Ultimately, up to 90 percent of the work of Level 1 analysts will be automated. 8. Collaborate: Security teams rely on coordination, collaboration, and effective communication. It is a team effort! The SOC cannot afford to ignore events. It must be a transparent workplace where all events

are fully processed through effective collaboration and linking of tools, people, processes, and automation. Cooperation must bring information, ideas and data to the forefront. The effect is that an SOC can further collaborate and invite professionals to contribute alerts, share critical time-sensitive details with colleagues, and share with practitioners to successfully address widespread threats.

9. Case management: Case management should be a core capability of the modern SOC. Even with the best efforts to prevent incidents, sometimes incidents happen. Security teams must have the skills and tools necessary to manage a response. Critical requirements for a SOC team include response plans, evidence collection, workflows, communication, timelines, and documentation.

10. Report: Today's world is data-driven, and security is not exempt. You can measure all aspects of the security process. Keep in mind that you cannot manage what you cannot measure. Using the right reporting tools will help measure and identify performance, track existing gaps, and define actions that security teams need to take now and in the future. A significant challenge for SOCs is the dependence on different platforms, which complicates accurate reporting.

In conclusion, the modern SOC should always provide real-time context on the threat landscape. Incorporating these capabilities makes the SOC a hyper-intelligent system that will offer transparency on threat environments, timely alerts, and context to assess an organization's security posture.

7

BLOCKCHAIN, AI & CYBERSECURITY

CHAPTER SEVEN

SECURITY LAWS IN EUROPE AND THE UNITED STATES

The history of cybersecurity regulation can be traced back to the 1990s, when the European Union passed the Data Protection Regulation. Soon after, the United States established a President's Commission on Critical Infrastructure Protection to identify and protect critical infrastructure, culminating in the 2001 National Strategy to Secure Cyberspace. Since then, Congress and the United States have passed numerous cybersecurity laws and regulations. The U.S. Department of Homeland Security (D.H.S.) created the U.S. Computer Emergency Response Team (US-CERT) to facilitate public-private sector information sharing on cyber threats. The U.S. Cyber Command was established in 2008 by the Secretary of Defense to protect U.S. national security interests.

The European Union recently passed the Global Data Protection Regulation (GDPR) in 2018 to add another layer of regulation to combat growing cybersecurity incidents and protect critical infrastructure. The European Union has some of the strictest data protection laws in the world. The passage of the GDPR has had far-reaching ramifications for companies around the world that, if found guilty, risk fines of up to 2 to 4 percent of their total global revenue. Since 2013, when the European Cybersecurity Strategy was approved, the European Union

has aggressively passed and enacted cybersecurity laws, particularly on data privacy, that most U.S. companies have not paid attention to. Most businesses, especially U.S. companies, are unaware of the European Union's cybersecurity frameworks, particularly the Network and Information Systems Security Directive, known as the N.I.S. Directive. The N.I.S. Directive, which came into force in 2016, authorizes European Union member states to regulate and enforce cybersecurity requirements within their borders. The passage of the Commission Communication to the European Parliament and Council has an annex and is intended to help member states implement the N.I.S. Directive. The directive applies to operators of essential services (O.E.S.) that are also critical infrastructure companies and digital service providers.

O.E.S. companies are required to meet the following requirements of the Directive:

- Implement all the technical and organizational security measures to prevent risks and manage the security of the network and information system.
- Notify the relevant national authorities of any serious cybersecurity incidents.

On the other hand, the directive imposed several obligations on EU member states, including:

- The development of a cybersecurity strategy;

- The establishment of a national point of contact for coordination with other member states; - Establishing cybersecurity incident response teams (CSIRTs) to help monitor events at the national level to provide early warnings and alerts on incidents at the national level to provide early warnings and alerts on incidents, respond to incidents, and share information among stakeholders;

- Assign the compliance monitoring role to the national competent authorities. These authorities will regularly verify that enterprises in EU member states are managing cybersecurity risks to their systems and networks. EU member states may set more stringent requirements than those already established by the EU;
- Ensure that U.S. companies minimize the impact of incidents and promptly notify national authorities or the CSIRT;

- Ensure that the relevant national authorities have the power and resources to assess whether O.E.S. companies are in compliance with the N.I.S. Directive, compel O.E.S. companies to provide critical information needed for assessment and implementation testing, and to issue binding instructions to the O.E.S. company to help address deficiencies.

The N.I.S. directive applies to U.S. companies operating in European Union member states. This means that U.S. companies must implement and comply with the security requirements of the regulations, hand over operational data to national authorities for conformity assessment, and provide corrective measures. Failure to comply will result in fines and penalties set by member states. The varying levels of N.I.S. enforcement by member states make it difficult for U.S. companies to comply.

On the other side of the world, the U.S. Congress passed the Clarifying Lawful Overseas Use of Data Act (CLOUD Act), which gives law enforcement agencies the right to obtain personal data from IT companies even when they are located in data servers in other countries. Other regulations and laws are in the pipeline, and their enactment could result in another wave of change for the cybersecurity industry.

In short, the cybersecurity strategies of the European Union focus on:
- Establishing a coherent international policy for cyberspace;
- Achieving cyber resilience;
- Reducing cybercrime;
- Develop industrial and technological resources for cybersecurity;
- Develop a cyber defense policy.

The United States cybersecurity strategies, instead, focus on:
- Creating a cyber-skilled workforce;
- Protecting critical infrastructure;
- Improve threat identification and reporting capabilities;
- Engage with international partners to promote Internet freedom;
- Secure federal networks.

The European Union and the United States do not have common

standards and certification legislation. Each jurisdiction has identified different policy areas and developed approaches that meet its specific needs. In the United States, the focus for cybersecurity standards has been on the NIST Framework, a set of voluntary standards published in 2014 and intended to improve the security of critical infrastructure. In the European Union, the European Commission is focusing on cohesive cybersecurity laws, which is why it developed the N.I.S. Directive. The directive requires all EU member states to adhere to a set of standards and always be adequately prepared before, during and after a cybersecurity breach.

Despite divergent approaches to cybersecurity laws and regulations, one area of consensus was the importance of public-private information sharing. The role of information sharing in preventing and mitigating attacks was recognized, particularly by digital service providers (D.S.P.) and operators of essential services (O.E.S.). The GDPR and the N.I.S. Directive have made it mandatory for data controllers and data processors. In addition, HEOs must immediately report cybersecurity breaches to data protection authorities. In the United States, the Cybersecurity Information Sharing Act (CISA) makes it easier for companies to monitor cybersecurity threats, implement defensive measures, and share information with other companies and the federal government.

In conclusion, policy discussions between the European Union and the United States will lay the groundwork for strong cooperation, especially on emerging cybersecurity trends and the protection of an open and interoperable Internet.

8

BLOCKCHAIN, AI & CYBERSECURITY

CHAPTER EIGHT

5G AND MACHINE LEARNING IMPACT ON CYBERSECURITY

8.1. THE DEPLOYMENT OF 5G AND ITS IMPACT ON CYBERSECURITY

The deployment of 5G will transform the way people live and work. Countries and companies alike are racing to deploy the fastest and largest 5G networks. Although 5G is still in its infancy, it has enormous potential to spur the creation of transformative new technologies and the development of new industries.

5G networks are designed to provide high data rates, increased reliability, ultra-low latency, huge network capacity, higher availability, and a better user experience. 5G will connect virtually everything and everyone with high performance and efficiency.

The greatest beneficiaries of the inherently high data rates and excellent network reliability will be businesses and organizations. Businesses will improve efficiency immensely and provide users with faster access to information and better experiences.

Once fully deployed, 5G is expected to transform sectors such as energy and electricity, healthcare, ICT, logistics, defense and many

others to promote initiatives/projects such as smart healthcare and telemedicine, smart factories and manufacturing, smart cities and smart transportation. Early adopters of technology will seek to take full advantage of the potential of Big Data, Cloud, AI and IoT to drive transformation. 5G will integrate these technologies and slowly abandon traditional network services.

Certainly, the widespread adoption of 5G in the coming years/decades will not be without challenges. 5G will be the backbone of increasingly digitized economies and societies. Innovation in the software and services supported by 5G and the role of vendors in building and operating 5G networks are identified as crucial security challenges.

5G will present unique cybersecurity challenges as it will connect billions of devices, objects and systems. Think of connected devices in critical industries and infrastructures such as banking, energy, healthcare and transportation, as well as critical industrial control systems carrying sensitive information. The need to improve security and build resilience of 5G networks is pertinent. Here, there are the key points of the impact of 5G for cybersecurity:

- Attack surfaces will potentially expand, thereby increasing exposure and presenting unique challenges for cybersecurity teams. 5G networks will be software-based, and cybercriminals will seek to exploit flaws such as low software development processes to insert backdoors.

- Compromised IoT-based DDoS attacks and those targeting endpoint/device application vulnerabilities will increase dramatically as 5G networks become widespread. Security experts predict that DDoS protection will be the most significant security challenge for 5G. The number of devices connected to the network will grow significantly and increase the risk of exploit attacks. Organizations and enterprises must invest in their vulnerability management capabilities to prevent large-scale DDoS attacks and ensure network integrity.

- Network equipment and functions will become increasingly sensitive due to the nature of 5G network architecture and new capabilities.

- Network availability and integrity, especially for critical installations and IT applications, will become a national security issue. Governments will be increasingly attentive to security challenges as 5G becomes a crucial backbone for various IT applications.

- The reliance on suppliers by mobile network operators will expose them to numerous risks and avenues of attack exploited by malicious actors. Countries have been wary of government-backed equipment vendors and have classified certain companies as potential threat actors in the deployment of 5G networks. The risk profile of a single vendor will need to be evaluated and taken into account when deploying 5G networks to mitigate exposure.

- Dependence on a single vendor increases the risk of exposure to outages. Vendors may experience business failures and related consequences, thus increasing vulnerabilities and exploitation by threat actors.

- Confidentiality and privacy threats will greatly increase when network availability and integrity are compromised.

Conventional approaches to security will not be sufficient with 5G networks. These challenges create a new security paradigm that requires a reevaluation of existing security policies and frameworks. At a minimum, organizations will need to employ scalable and automated security solutions to protect networks and data. Security solutions must be supported by artificial intelligence (AI)- and machine learning (ML)-based threat detection and response capabilities. In addition, security challenges can be addressed by adopting security models shared by enterprises and network operators.

8.2. A POTENTIAL VULNERABILITY TO CYBERATTACKS: 5G NETWORK SLICING

An important security flaw in the 5G network architecture has been identified. The network slicing flaws impacts virtualized network functions and can enable data theft and denial of service attacks. A significant vulnerability between different network slices of a 5G operator can leave enterprise customers exposed to malicious cyberattacks.

AdaptiveMobile Security was the first entity to discover the flaw and shared its findings with the GSM Association (GSMA) on February 4, 2021. The GSMA designated the 5G network weaknesses collectively as CVD-2021-0047.

5G is a step forward from the current 4G broadband network technology. 5G is a service-based architecture (SBA) that works by providing a modular framework that deploys a set of related network functions.

5G enables consumers to discover and authorize access to a plethora of services. Network functions are responsible for managing sessions, registering subscribers, storing subscriber data, managing subscriber profiles, and connecting users to the Internet via a base station. Each network function of the SBA can offer a specific service and at the same time request a service from another network function.

The 5G SBA is a new network concept that opens the network to new partners and services, presenting unique security challenges. The slicing model is one of the most significant ways in which the SBA core of the 5G network is composed. Each slice within the core network carries a logical group of network functions assigned exclusively to that specific slice or shared among several slices. The creation of separate slices that prioritize unique features, such as large bandwidths, allows a network operator to offer customized solutions to particular industries.

The identified network issue is most likely to cause significant security risks to businesses that depend on network slicing and further undermine operators' attempts to open up new revenue from 5G. The risk of attack is still low due to the small number of mobile operators with multiple active network slicing on their networks. Efforts are ongoing among mobile security vendors, the GSMA, network operators and regulators to address 5G network slicing and undertake architecture updates to prevent exploitation.

5G network slicing allows mobile operators to divide their core and radio networks into multiple distinct virtual blocks designed to provide different amounts of resources and priorities to different types of traffic. For example, a mobile broadband network slice can offer entertainment and internet services, while the Internet of Things (IoT) slice offers specific services for retail and manufacturing. In contrast, low-latency autonomous slices can be used for mission-critical activities such as healthcare.

Network partitioning is a distinctive feature of 5G. It allows network operators to make sections of their core network available for specific vertical use cases such as automotive, critical infrastructure, entertainment and healthcare. The effect is that the network opens up to numerous partners after being divided into blocks and specific vertical use cases.

An examination of 5G core networks carrying both shared and dedicated network functions by AdaptiveMobile Security indicates that networks supporting hybrid network functions with multiple slices experience a lack of mapping between transport and application layer identities.

This serious flaw in industry standards could have widespread repercussions, creating an opportunity for attackers to perpetrate data breaches and launch multi-layer denial of service attacks after gaining access to the 5G service-based architecture. The situation is serious and could encourage hackers to exploit the network design flaw in the slicing standard and gain access to the operator's core network and network slices assigned to other companies. In fact, network operators and their customers will be exposed and risk losing sensitive location data. Stolen location data can be used to track a user's location, lose pricing information, and potentially cause disruption to slices and network functions. The mobile phone industry is implementing 5G network technology with the intention of increasing efficiency and improving functionality. The transition to 5G is inevitable because it brings many benefits.

However, a change in mindset and the adoption of holistic and collaborative measures are needed to address network security challenges. Concerted efforts are needed from working groups, standards bodies, network operators and vendors.

Further research is needed to determine whether the mechanisms of the currently defined 5G standards are sufficient to stop attackers. The process revealed that the following major attack scenarios cannot be prevented at present with the network slicing flaw, such as:

- Extraction of user data;
- Access to network functions and information belonging to vertical clients;
- Denial of service.

Core networks are moving toward IT- and cloud-based architecture, and hacking tools are becoming increasingly available to malicious actors. The impact of the network slicing vulnerability on real-world applications is limited to the number of slices within 5G networks. The associated risks would have been significant had the fundamental flaw in 5G standards remained undiscovered. AdaptiveMobile Security recommends countermeasures that include dividing the network into different security zones and applying security filters for signaling between different slices, the core network and external partners, as well as shared and unshared network functions.

It is necessary to include signaling layer protection solutions to protect against data leakage attacks that exploit the lack of correlation between application and transport layers. Having alerted the industry to the severity of the 5G network breach, it is essential to promote best practices in the future, together with all stakeholders.

8.3. THE IMPACT OF MACHINE LEARNING (ML) ON COMPANIES AND INDUSTRIES

Numerous companies in different industries have struggled during the COVID-19 pandemic. There were a few exceptions, especially in the field of information technology, which revealed unnecessary duplication and waste. The move to remote work was one such move that exposed inefficiencies and other waste.

The use of technologies such as data science and machine learning has ensured that companies remain lean and efficient in these challenging times. Trials to adopt these technologies had already begun before the coronavirus outbreak. The COVID-19 pandemic helped accelerate the adoption of these technologies as companies scrambled to cope.

Machine learning uses powerful algorithms to draw insights from real-world data and make predictions about future outcomes. The availability of new data makes it easier to refine machine learning programs and make better, up-to-date predictions. Keep in mind that machine learning is not a perfect solution, just like other tools. However, machine learning outperforms various statistical and linear algorithms in most situations.

Below are the most common areas where machine learning is making a big difference: - Where experts cannot code the rules - Human-oriented tasks present unique challenges that are not easily solved through simple or deterministic rule-based solutions. In some functions, many factors influence the final answer, which means that engineers would have to repeatedly write and update a huge number of lines of code.

In addition, it is difficult to code precise rules that depend on too many overlapping factors or need fine-tuning. Machine learning comes into play mainly because ML programs require only appropriate algorithms to automatically extract patterns:

- When scaling to millions of cases, for example, one may be able to manually classify a few hundred payments as fraudulent. However, it becomes impossible when dealing with millions of payments to sift through and mark as fraudulent. Organizations adopt artificial intelligence-based solutions when their user base grows and manual processing becomes impossible. Users increasingly need quick responses, especially for monetary matters. They no longer want to wait minutes or hours before getting satisfactory answers to their queries. Machine learning offers the tools to handle large-scale data problems without the need for human intervention.

- For handling manual tasks when it is not cost-efficient - There are manual tasks that can be handled by an organization's staff quickly and effectively. However, the manual workload is often associated with a high cost in terms of time and operational costs. Machine learning offers a well-defined and optimized method of processing data and other tasks. ML technology helps reduce the time and budgets associated with completing various jobs. In many cases, machine learning offers a predictable, consumption-based pricing strategy, even for fully scaled operations.

- To handle massive datasets that have not obvious patterns - It is not uncommon to have a well-chosen data set and know the underlying problem. However, one is confused by the inability to identify explicit patterns from the data. The lack of obvious marks may have prevented any validation from being coded.

In addition, there could be typographical errors, missing fields, and even human error, but no validation was done. You may also know that the dataset is of poor quality and manually complete the missing entries or affected rows. However, no connection can be made between valid and invalid records.

Machine learning algorithms can help detect any distinguishable patterns and solve the problem. These algorithms can quickly establish any hidden connections between data points that the human eye cannot pick up. Some machine learning tools also explain how they arrived at their connections and validations.

- Enhance adaptability in an ever-changing world - The world is changing more and more, as are rapid changes in technology. This implies that problems solved yesterday can easily change. A previous solution, which may become useless or inefficient, must be modified accordingly. For example, an organization that processes medical appointment records for different uses, such as diagnoses, billing codes, and procedure information, will need to regularly review its rules. Required updates cannot be implemented in real time. Errors and mislabeled entries can lead to legal consequences, large fines

and insurance rejections.

Machine learning ensures that models and other learning methods can be collected from data throughout the application lifecycle. Machine learning learns from the first line of code to the end of the model. It ensures that production systems can have feedback loops that help immediately detect problems that the model fails to solve correctly.

In conclusion, remember that machine learning is a tool and not a magic solution. Machine learning is about creating models that use advanced mathematical algorithms to identify patterns in the data and offer validations or additional learning points. When used appropriately in different situations, machine learning can help reduce time spent on tasks, eliminate errors associated with manual IT operations, reduce IT costs, and increase business value.

9

BLOCKCHAIN, AI & CYBERSECURITY

CHAPTER NINE

ARTIFICIAL INTELLIGENCE (AI) IN CYBERSECURITY AND OTHER SECTORS

9.1. AI AND ML FOR CYBERSECURITY

Artificial intelligence (AI) in cybersecurity introduces a proactive way to fight cyber threats. Together with machine learning (ML), AI is now an essential tool for cybersecurity. AI is crossing aspects of cybersecurity, with organizations and security teams relying on technology to fight off threats. Analytics, a necessary technological capability of AI, has helped analyze data and risk behaviors from millions of cyber incidents to identify potential cyber threats and strange events on employee accounts. In real time, analytics helps security teams take timely action to block threats. In addition, AI helps ensure business continuity in the event of an attack.

AI algorithms become as useful as the humans behind the technology. Cybersecurity professionals must harness the potential of AI by understanding how it can be used in data analysis to detect potential threats and inform next actions. Cybercriminals will stop at nothing in creating and modifying malware code to evade detection by security software and methods. It is a never-ending struggle between defenders and attackers.

Identifying every variation of malware is not easy as cybercriminals become increasingly intelligent and sophisticated. The use of AI and ML allows defenders to stay ahead of the curve, enabling them to block unknown and new types of malware and cyber threats.

ML is particularly useful for solving unknown or not-so-explicit threats. It can be the basis for creating anti-malware solutions, as it can tap into the machine learning database of previously detected threats. The new form of malware can be checked against the database by examining the code, identifying it, and blocking the attack. The same applies to cases where malicious code has been embedded within delicate pieces of code to hide the intent of the delivered payload. Machine learning techniques have been successful in discovering attacks and protecting users from new malware campaigns.

In addition to discovering new malware variants, AI and ML can be used to augment cybersecurity efforts. An AI-based network monitoring tool is one such method used to track the daily activities of network users. By developing a clear picture of typical behavior, the information is used by cybersecurity teams to detect risky practices and act accordingly to protect the network, users and sensitive data. This means that if an employee clicks on a phishing link, the system will detect it as abnormal behavior and flag it as potential malicious activity.

Artificial intelligence is about the ability to adapt and respond to the changing cybersecurity landscape. AI helps defenders understand the relevance of cybersecurity measures, the consequences of a breach, changes in behavior, react intelligently, and develop a proportional response to attacks in real time.

AI and ML have given companies agility and flexibility to detect, prevent, respond to, and recover from cyber attacks. With ML, companies can detect threats, block malicious intrusions, prevent malware distribution, and prevent data theft. All of this can be done without compromising the day-to-day operations of the company. In addition, a network does not have to be shut down if malicious activity is detected on a single machine. A timely and proportionate response can be injected to prevent the disruption of daily activities and decision-making processes.

Not only that, AI- and ML-based security tools can be programmed incorrectly, causing algorithms to miss critical indicators of a potential cyber threat. Serious problems can arise if a device has not been coded to account for specific parameters. Therefore, any artificial intelligence security tool is only as useful as the people working on it. Keep in mind that cybercriminals can also use these technologies to escape detection and become more effective in launching attacks. Of course AI and ML cybersecurity technology does not replace cybersecurity personnel within the organization. AI will not solve all cybersecurity problems. The use of technology must be anchored in experience and continuous adaptation by security personnel. Artificial intelligence will not replace security personnel, who will need to assess and adapt patterns to detect vulnerabilities more quickly and prevent attacks.

Artificial intelligence is an emerging technology that is feared to make cyber threats more dangerous and harder to detect. Cybercriminals may have already started using AI to carry out their nefarious actions. AI-based deepfake technology has already caused a stir in the cybersecurity industry as it has been used to spread misinformation or abuse people through fake videos. Cybercriminals have used AI-generated audio to impersonate a CEO and fool employees' voices to transfer about $240,000. It has become an arms race between defenders and attackers in the use of AI technology.

Finally, the development and improvement of AI-based cybersecurity tools and their proper use by security teams will help protect companies from smart and powerful cyber threats.

9.2. AI IN THE EDUCATION AND FINANCE SECTOR

Market Research Engine's latest findings indicate that the global AI market in education will reach $5.8 billion by 2025. Overall, AI is revolutionizing the way teaching and learning happens.

Here, there is how AI is changing the education sector:

- Task automation. AI has great potential in automating administrative functions, making the work of educational institutions and teachers easier. Both teachers and professors are forced to handle organizational

and administrative tasks in addition to teaching. These non-teaching tasks can be overwhelming and include executive and administrative activities such as managing teaching materials, organizing teaching resources and preparing periodic progress reports.

According to recent research, teachers spend 43% of their time on teaching, 13% on lesson planning, 11% on test taking, and 7%on administrative tasks. Task automation will enable teachers to save time spent on non-teaching activities, including managing administrative work and correcting tests. Teachers can become more productive and devote time to individual sessions with students.

- Smart content. Artificial intelligence is expected to add new methods for learning and success. Smart content involves different types of virtual content, such as digitized guides, video lectures and video conferencing. The creation of customizable learning interfaces and digital content will improve learning outcomes. Students will be able to learn faster, access materials efficiently and achieve academic goals.

Smart data collection, supported by intelligent computer systems, is helping academic institutions better engage with current and potential students. It is interesting to see how data mining systems play an integral role in higher education, but artificial intelligence could be the key. Artificial intelligence will help recruit students, choose the best courses, and provide students with a college/school experience tailored to their needs and goals.

- Differentiated and personalized learning. Students are different and have different approaches to learning. Through personalized instruction, students can improve their academic achievement regardless of their starting level. AI will help make learning content easier to assimilate by offering specific recommendations and feedback to improve learning performance and effectiveness.

The use of AI tools will help track progress and generate impact reports that will further help create relevant materials for students. Personalized learning will have a more significant impact on students with disabilities in learning and content absorption.

The use of artificial intelligence can help trial-and-error learning become less intimidating for students. The idea of failure can sometimes become very overwhelming. Some students fear being put in the spotlight in front of their peers or teachers and having to face questions or other learning tasks. A computer system based on artificial intelligence can help students learn in a less daunting environment. Students can learn in an environment that is free of judgment and supports learning by trial and error. The AI-based system will provide solutions to questions and enable improved learning outcomes.

We may see AI become more sophisticated and develop machines that can read students' facial expressions. They could help identify times when a student struggles to grasp a concept or topic and then modify the lesson appropriately to make the idea better understood. Although the idea of tailoring a curriculum to each student's needs is not currently feasible, it could be an area where AI-powered machines could provide solutions.

- Virtual Learning Environment. Artificial intelligence powers the platforms used to digitize textbooks and enable access through devices. These platforms enable students who cannot attend classes to study and foreign students to study courses not available in their countries. Artificial intelligence makes it possible to translate learning materials into different languages, which is useful for non-English speakers. Virtual learning is providing opportunities for more and more students. Students can now learn virtually anywhere without the need to be physically present in the classroom.

- Universal access and 24/7 support. AI chatbots in education have helped students answer any questions without waiting for class time. AI chatbots act as 24-hour assistants, allowing students to resolve their questions anytime and from anywhere.

- Facial Recognition: Some academic institutions have reportedly begun using AI-driven facial scans to identify their students. Facial recognition eliminates the need for student IDs and improves administrative, research, and security activities. The technology can also prevent crimes within academic institutions, as it can be used to identify perpetrators.

The increase in violence and gun-related incidents in schools has forced school administrators and other security actors to find ways to combat these threats. Increased investment in artificial intelligence-based surveillance and security solutions will help counter school shootings and other crimes.

- A change in the role of teachers: Teachers will always have a role to play in education. The teacher is irreplaceable! However, the increasing use of artificial intelligence in education may herald a change in the role of the teacher. Artificial intelligence may take on functions such as correcting tests, improving student performance, and helping with real-world tutoring. As AI technologies continue to drive changes in the classroom, we will continue to see a modification of teachers' roles, but never a total replacement of them.

Both Artificial Intelligence and Blockchain technology are changing the field of education forever. We can manage the change by developing specialized training for teachers, professors and education managers. It will be challenging, but the process has begun and cannot be stopped.

Even in the financial sector, financial service institutions are moving themselves from experimentation to implementation of artificial intelligence (AI) and machine learning (ML). We are increasingly seeing large-scale adoption of these technologies.

The benefits are a reduction in the need for manual intervention in their operations, improved security, and the freeing up of resources and time for continuous innovation. AI and ML technologies have promised long-term value and strategic advantages, as well as significantly reducing the time between idea generation and business value creation. Traditional financial institutions, such as banks, are transforming into digitally oriented companies, developing the ability to constantly focus on customers, just like large technology companies.

Here, there are the areas can be improved through the adoption of AI and ML in the financial services sector:

- Document processing with intelligent automation. AI and ML technologies enable intelligent and robotic automation, helping to streamline various functions, improve the speed and accuracy of financial processes, increase overall efficiency, and lead to significant cost savings. For example, blockchain has been important in e-KYC (electronic know your customer). e-KYC is paperless and executed remotely, helping to reduce the bureaucratic costs of protocols used in KYC, such as verification of customer signatures and identities. Repetitive and mundane tasks and processes, such as document management, regulatory reporting, and loan disbursement and repayment, are gradually being automated. Financial organizations are using intelligent automation platforms to extract, manage and interpret unstructured data that includes scanned documents, text, images, faxes and web content. The natural language processing (NLP) engine, characterized by high levels of accuracy and reliability, helps identify unseen, missing and malformed data. As a result, average handling times are effectively reduced and companies gain a competitive advantage through a greatly improved customer experience.

- Thorough and efficient customer service. The use of virtual assistants helps financial organizations respond to customer needs with minimal employee input. Chatbots have become very popular on e-commerce sites, and similar solutions are expected to become popular in the financial services industry. Some organizations such as JP Morgan are using bots to streamline back-office operations and offer customer support. The net effect of using chatbots and virtual assistants has been an increase in productivity, a reduction in the time and effort required to answer generic customer questions, and the freeing up of teams for critical, long-term projects that will drive innovation.

All platforms used contract intelligence, abbreviated as COIN, which is based on machine learning systems. COIN automates legal filing tasks, examines documents and handles basic IT requests, such as password resets. Other uses of the technology include creating new tools for clients and bankers to reduce human error and provide more excellent expertise.

- Risk management analytics. Creditworthiness is estimated primarily by the likelihood of an individual or company to repay a loan. Risk management processes in all lending institutions are based on determining the probability of loan default. Even with impeccable data, this process presents challenges because some individuals and organizations are not truthful in stating their ability to pay-back a loan.

Financial companies such as ZestFinance and Lenddo have used AI to determine creditworthiness and risk assessment. Other examples include credit bureaus such as Equifax, which use AI and ML and advanced data tools to analyze alternative data sources to offer customer insights and assess risk.

The use of AI has enabled lending organizations to expand the limited data set for this process. AI has made it possible to analyze an individual's entire digital financial footprint to determine his or her creditworthiness and default risk, instead of traditionally using credit scores and annual salaries.

9.3. AI IN THE HEALTH CARE SECTOR

Over the past decade, we have seen an increase in the use of AI in the health sector. With the adoption of big data and AI in healthcare, the public has its hopes and fears about the use of healthcare data.

Here, there are some hopes of the use of AI in healthcare:
- Keeping healthy and well. The most significant benefit of AI has been to help people stay healthy and reduce hospital visits. We are seeing widespread use of AI and the Internet of Medical Things in consumer health applications that push people to live healthy lives. The apps encourage people to adopt healthier behaviors and play a proactive role in managing healthy lifestyles. AI is putting consumers in charge of their overall health and well-being. On the other hand, AI is helping healthcare providers better understand the daily needs and lifestyles of their clients/patients. With the information gathered, health care providers can offer better guidance, feedback, and support to stay healthy.
- Early detection and diafnosis. AI is offering advances in early detection of diseases such as cancer, accurately and in the early stages. The use of AI in the review and translation of mammograms leads to up to 99 percent accuracy of diagnosis and 30 times faster speed. In fact, it eliminates misdiagnoses and reduces unnecessary biopsies. The use of consumer wearables in combination with AI leads to detection of early-stage heart disease. These devices help physicians detect and prevent life-threatening episodes, perform effective monitoring, and treat the disease while it is still possible.
IBM's Watson for Health assists healthcare organizations in applying cognitive technology to unlock large amounts of health data and use it for diagnosis. Watson can examine and store large amounts of medical information from around the world faster than any human. Google's DeepMind Health helps health researchers, physicians and patients solve real-world health problems. The technology behind DeepMind employs machine learning and neuroscience to build learning algorithms that mimic the human brain.
- Decision making and treatment. Substantial improvements in health

care require aligning big data in health care with timely and decisive decisions. Predictive analytics using AI helps support decision making and clinical actions. Pattern recognition is used to identify patients at risk of developing diseases due to environmental factors, lifestyle choices, and genomic factors, which are carefully monitored and analyzed by AI.

In addition to scanning health data to identify those at risk, AI is increasingly being used to take a more comprehensive approach to disease management, improve coordination of care plans, and assist patients in managing and adhering to long-term treatment plans. AI has facilitated the increased use of robots in the medical field. We see very complex surgical robots assisting surgeons in the operating room or performing surgeries independently. Robots are also being used for repetitive tasks in hospitals and laboratories, for physical therapy, and to support people with chronic conditions.

People are living longer than previous generations, which increases the importance of end-of-life care. Robots have a huge impact on end-of-life care, particularly by improving independence and supporting people with heart failure, osteoporosis, and dementia. Advances in humanoid design will help support conversations and social interactions, keeping elderly minds sharp and eliminating loneliness.

- Research and training. Artificial intelligence plays a key role in shortening the path from research laboratories to patients, which is usually long and expensive. Applying AI in research and drug development to streamline processes and drug discovery effectively reduces the time between the lab and the market and lowers costs. Traditionally, it takes about 12 years for a new drug to move from the research laboratory to human use. Only 5 of the 5,000 drugs in development make it to the human trial stage, and developing a drug ready for human use costs about $360 million.

In training, AI is transforming learning as it can provide realistic simulations. AI can draw from many healthcare databases to inform decisions, answer questions, and offer advice to learners. AI improves learning outcomes and needs by building and adjusting based on prior challenges and responses. Finally, with AI, training can be conducted anywhere, not limited to a classroom or hospital setting.

In contrast, here are some fears that people have about AI in the health sector:

- Robots. Some people have a negative opinion about the use of robots in healthcare. The prevailing fear is that something could go

wrong with robots, causing intentional harm and risk to humans. Not all people would be ready to have a robot operate on them or interact with them during a hospital visit.

- Ethical issues. The increasing use of AI technology in healthcare may threaten patient preferences, privacy, and safety. Many people believe that AI is being used to monitor their behaviors, lifestyle choices, and health status. Privacy is a primary concern: people fear that their health data may be sold to third parties or used for purposes they do not agree with. There is an urgent need to identify ethical challenges and mitigate them. However, current ethical policies and guidelines for the use of AI in healthcare lag behind the advances made by AI in diagnosis, clinical decision-making, biomedical research, medical education, and robotics.

The COVID-19 pandemic has highlighted the importance of faster methods for drug discovery and development. New variants of disease-causing pathogens can cause immeasurable harm before new effective treatments are discovered. The emergence of new technologies is helping to speed up the discovery process until new drugs are approved. These work only if they can adhere to target protein molecules in the body. Machine learning and artificial intelligence are helping to speed up the calculations needed to determine the binding affinity of drug molecules to proteins in the body.

Scientists are employing a new technique called DeepBAR to calculate the binding affinity between drug candidates and targets. Using this approach, the time of the development and approval processes can be greatly reduced by precise calculations made in a fraction of the time taken by previous methods. According to medical and pharmaceutical professionals, DeepBAR should help speed up critical protein engineering and drug discovery processes. According to Bin Zhang, Pfizer-Laubach Career Development Professor in Chemistry at MIT and an associate member of the Broad Institute at MIT and Harvard, the new method is many times faster than previous methods. This means that DeepBAR can provide an efficient and reliable method for drug discovery.

The affinity between drug molecules and target proteins is measured using a quantity referred to as binding free energy. The value obtained should be lower, as it represents the closest binding between the drug molecule and the target protein. A lower binding free energy implies that the drug being discovered is able to complete the target site better than other molecules, increasing the chances of disrupting the normal functions of that protein.

9.4. THE FASCINATING WORLD OF ARTIFICIAL INTELLIGENCE

Among the various nuances of Artificial Intelligence is that of its integration with 5G. The combination of 5G and AI is expected to transform the world as we know it in industry, business and personal levels. 5G is designed to offer higher peak data rates and multi-Gbps, higher reliability, ultra-low latency, massive network capacity, consistent user experiences and higher availability.

In this regard, Researchers at Incheon National University in South Korea are addressing the problems associated with an AI-based, 5G-integrated virtual emotion recognition system called 5G-I-VEmoSYS. The 5G-I-VEmoSYS is used to detect human emotions through body movements and wireless signals. The results of the study led by Prof. Hyunbum Kim have been published in IEEE Network. Emotions are a fundamental human characteristic that helps differentiate humans from machines. Emotions generally define everyday human activities. However, some emotions are not exactly useful and can disrupt the daily functioning of society and endanger people's lives. For example, an unstable driver on the road poses a significant threat to the lives and well-being of other road users.

The emergence and use of emotion detection technology have immense potential to identify and recognize disruptive emotions and alert affected people to the potential danger. Emotion detection technology can be used with 5G and even beyond 5G communication. According to Prof. Kim, an AI-enabled car guidance system can alert pedestrians and other road users of impending danger in the case of an unstable driver. The system will use the nearest network towers to warn the nearest pedestrians and other drivers of the impending danger to their devices.

5G-I-VEmoSYS can recognize five different types of emotions, including joy, anger, pleasure, sadness, and a neutral state. The system architecture includes three subsystems that will handle the detection, flow, and mapping of human emotions. Here's how it works:

- One system, the Artificial Intelligence Virtual Emotion Barrier or AI-VEmoBAR, plays the role of sensing by relying on the reflection of a

human's wireless signals to detect his or her emotions.
- The second system is the Artificial Intelligence Virtual Emotion Flow, or AI- VEmoFLOW, which receives emotion information and facilitates the flow of specific emotion information at specific times and particular areas.

- Lastly, the Artificial Intelligence Virtual Emotion Map or AI-VEmoMAP will use large amounts of virtual emotion data to create a virtual emotion map that will help detect threats and prevent crimes. Overall, the most significant advantage of 5G-I-VEmoSYS is that it can complete emotion detection without revealing the face or other private elements of subjects. The system can protect the privacy of citizens, especially in public areas. In private spaces, 5G-I-VEmoSYS allows users to choose whether to remain anonymous or reveal their identity when providing information to the system. Despite the privacy issue, the system will immediately transmit information to the relevant authorities to detect deep emotions such as fear and anger. The police department or other authorities will take necessary measures to prevent crimes or other threats such as terrorism.
Beyond emotions, artificial intelligence can identify weaknesses and influence human choices. This happens because modern AI is brilliant. In practice, there are an increasing number of breakthrough discoveries concerning how AI can interact with and on humans. For example, recent findings reveal that AI can learn to identify weaknesses in human behavior and use the data to influence decision making.
And indeed, AI can learn to influence human behavior. Researchers at CSIRO Data61, the data and digital branch of Australia's national science agency, have developed a method to identify and exploit vulnerabilities in decision-making. The team used a recurrent neural network and deep reinforcement learning to find and exploit human weaknesses.
The model was tested through three experiments that required human participants to play against a computer.
The first experiment required participants to click on red or blue colored boxes to win some fake coin. Artificial intelligence learned the participants' choice patterns and guided them toward a specific choice. The study indicated that artificial intelligence was successful in 70% of the cases. The second experiment involved participants looking at a screen and pressing a button when a particular symbol, an orange triangle, appeared on the screen. Other participants were not required to press the button if another symbol, such as a blue circle, appeared on the screen. Again, the AI tried to arrange a sequence of symbols that would force participants to make

more mistakes. Similarly, the results showed an increase of about 25 percent in the number of errors. Lastly, the third experiment involved participating in several rounds in which one pretended to be an investor distributing money to a trustee. The trustee, in this case, is the AI. The AI then returns some of the money to the participant, who decides how much to invest in the next round. The game was played in two different modes: the first required the AI to maximize the amount of money it had available. The second mode involved the AI achieving an equal distribution of money between itself and the human investor. In each case, the AI was able to achieve its intended results.

In each of the experiments, AI learned from the participants' responses, identifying and targeting vulnerabilities in human decision-making. In the end, the machine learned how to influence and direct participants to complete a specific action.

Although the results are based on small and unrealistic situations, they indicate a direction that could be pursued using AI. Further research is needed to determine how AI can be used to identify weaknesses and influence people's choices for the benefit of society. The results of this research promote a better understanding of what AI can do and also how people make their choices. In addition, the study reveals how machines can learn and help influence choices through everyday interactions with humans.

Facial recognition based on artificial intelligence also continues its development path at a rapid pace. Facial recognition is becoming mainstream. Daily application of this technology includes unlocking devices and even tagging friends on Facebook. It is considered one of the most natural biometric technologies available today. After all, we recognize ourselves by looking at our faces. As the technology develops further, serious concerns and reactions arise. Facial recognition refers to the identification and verification of an individual's identity through the use of his or her face. Facial recognition captures, analyzes and compares distinct patterns based on the details of an individual's face. Facial biometrics transforms a face into digital data by applying an algorithm and comparing the captured image with those in a database. Facial biometrics is the preferred benchmark for biometrics because it is quick and easy to implement. Another advantage is that there is no physical interaction with the end user.

Here, there are the major trends in facial recognition that have defined the landscape in 2021:

- Rapid refinement of facial recognition technologies. Major software giants are engaged in a race for biometric innovation, with projects published and launched in the areas of artificial intelligence, facial analysis, and image recognition.
Projects by major IT giants, such as Academia's GaussianFace, have achieved a facial identification rate of 98.52 percent, Facebook and Google's DeepFace has an accuracy rate of 97.53 percent, and Amazon's Rekognition has been used by law enforcement agencies to make comparisons between faces and databases.
Further developments in the field include facial emotion recognition (FER), which seeks to map facial expressions to identify emotions such as anger, joy, disgust, surprise, sadness and a host of compound emotions.
Further developments will involve the recognition and interpretation of human emotions. In addition to facial detection/recognition, other applications include facial expression detection and the expression of specific emotional states.

- Deep learning. Deep learning is the technology that helps the system learn from data. Deep learning is central to the development of current algorithms that help face detection, face tracking, face matching, and real-time translation of conversations. This technology helps improve facial recognition systems. Artificial neural network algorithms are further improving the accuracy of facial recognition algorithms.

- Expanding facial recognition markets. The global facial recognition market is estimated to generate revenues of about $7 billion by 2024. The industry's growth is driven by numerous applications. The main growth driver is surveillance in the public sector.

The top three applications of facial recognition involve law enforcement to combat crime and terrorism by tracking and identifying criminals. Facial recognition is used for issuing identity documents in combination with other biometric technologies. Police departments use facial biometrics to search databases of driver's licenses and passport photos.

In the health sector, facial analysis and deep learning enable accurate tracking of patients' medication use, detection of genetic diseases, and support of pain management procedures. Facial recognition in the retail and banking sectors is the most promising. The application of facial recognition is in the KYC (Know Your Customer) sector, which gained more importance during the pandemic. Banks have moved to digital account opening and other digital onboarding channels. The retail sector is testing facial recognition payment solutions, which are at an advanced stage of development.

- Facial recognition hackers. Hacking and data theft are of increasing concern in the field of facial recognition. Hacking incidents are on the rise, even though technical and legal measures have been taken to protect data, privacy and people from these crimes.

A Russian man, Grigory Bakunov, has developed an algorithm that helps people avoid proper facial recognition by confusing face detection devices. The algorithm creates a unique trick that is used to fool facial recognition software. However, the algorithm has not been put on the market to prevent criminals from using it for nefarious purposes.

A Berlin-based artist, Adam Harvey, has created a CV Dazzle device that works similarly to the previously described solution. In addition, the artist is working on clothing with patterns that help prevent facial recognition. The key is the incorporating fabric patterns such as eyes and mouths that help fool any facial recognition system. German researchers revealed a hack that allowed them to bypass Windows 10 Hello facial authentication by printing an infrared facial image.

A fascinating experiment by Thomas Smith, published recently in January, brought to the forefront a simple technique that could help make oneself invisible to facial recognition systems. By wearing a disposable mask and opaque sunglasses, an individual can quickly become invisible to these systems.

- The moral and ethical conundrum. A central question that needs to be fully answered is whether it is worth risking users' privacy in exchange for security and efficiency. Facial recognition is stirring controversy, especially because of the racial undertones involved. In the United Kingdom, the Court of Appeal has banned the use of

this technology in law enforcement, arguing that it violates data protection, human rights, and equality laws.

Police brutality and racially motivated law enforcement practices in the United States have seen major IT giants such as IBM, Amazon and Microsoft distance themselves from the development and sale of facial recognition technology to law enforcement. The biggest threat is privacy, as people do not want their faces recorded without permission and stored in databases for unknown future use. Real-time facial recognition surveillance by law enforcement has been banned in many cities and some countries. It is argued that law enforcement officers would check people in their databases without a warrant, as if they were treating people as criminals for no reason. Facial recognition in these cases violates human rights and personal rights.

9.5. AI FOR GOVERNMENTS: BETWEEN IT GIANTS AND GENERAL LACK OF TRUST

Governments around the world are embracing artificial intelligence with great enthusiasm in an effort to stay abreast of technological advances. Both governments and companies are keen to include artificial intelligence in their business development processes and other applications.

More than 22 countries have already developed and launched their national strategies on AI to incorporate it into business development. In addition, ethical frameworks have been formulated to guide the development of AI technologies. In the European Union alone, more than 290 policy initiatives on AI have been launched in member states between 2016 and 2020.

The most recent strategy on AI was launched in Ireland and was aptly named "AI - Here for Good." In the strategy, Ireland outlined how it intends to become an international leader in using AI to improve the economy and society. Through an ethical and people-centered approach, Ireland seeks to adopt AI for its own development. Ireland aims to promote the adoption of AI by Irish businesses and government agencies through an ethical and moral framework. Experts pointed out that the strategy has some shortcomings, just like strategies adopted by other countries that do not address the wrong AI strategies, such as unwarranted surveillance.

The strategies adopted by some countries merely join the bandwagon of hype and hysteria that accompanied the adoption of AI. There is a widespread notion that AI is one of the most important developments in human history, on par with fire and electricity. Ireland's AI strategy follows the wave of hype, claiming that the technology can double economic growth by 2035. No details were given as to how this could be achieved using AI. In fact, large multinational corporations such as Google have changed their business model to reflect dependence on AI. According to Sundar Pichai, CEO of Google's parent company, Alphabet, the company's business model depends on AI and people's trust in the technology. AI is critical to the operation and performance of digital platforms, including Amazon, Google, Facebook, Alibaba and Apple. These large multinational companies enjoy a winner-takes-all approach due to big data and first-mover advantage. The profitability of these platforms increases with the exponential growth of data collected and by simply being the first to get it right. Unfortunately, these companies have taken on monopolistic tendencies and become gatekeepers to the AI industry.

The Irish strategy praises some of the AI-based apps that have made a significant impact. One such app helped improve Dublin's cycling infrastructure. Other AI-based apps popular in Ireland provide Irish language tools, comfort people with dementia, and help save energy in businesses and households. From these applications of AI, it becomes difficult to see how they can help double economic growth. On the contrary, large digital platforms have negatively affected existing businesses, overtaking them in competition, sometimes unfairly. A notable example is the way Google has dominated and disrupted the advertising industry and overtaken the traditional newspaper model; even Apple has managed to sell more watches than the traditional Swiss watch industry.

Not only that, even start-ups have found it difficult to thrive amid the growing competition from these IT giants. This has led to stifling innovation in the industry, as entrepreneurs cannot compete with all these platforms. The competitive landscape is heavily skewed toward the large digital platforms.

In an effort to address these abuses, the EU has prepared proposals for a Digital Markets Act (DMA) and Digital Services Act (DSA).

Some of the great promises of automation and AI as an unrepeatable invention have yet to be realized. On the contrary, we have witnessed phenomena contrary to the projections of exponential labor productivity and rising unemployment due to the widespread adoption of AI.

Most AI strategies adopted by several countries, including Ireland, ignore the challenges listed above. Most of the strategies do not refer to the big digital platforms such as Amazon, Google and Facebook, do not mention platform capitalism, the antitrust actions taken against Google by the EU, the DSA and the DMA.

Finally, there is precisely a lack of trust in AI that is never addressed in these strategies. In most cases, the lack of trust has been attributed to a lack of understanding of the technology. An effort should be made to teach people about AI and data science. However, it is feared that the more people understand AI, the more they do not trust the technology. Lack of trust even on the part of companies has led to low adoption rates, amid fears that AI does not make business sense, with paltry returns and very high environmental impact.

AI is not a magic wand that can be waved over problems. Any strategy must take into account data protection, privacy, and carbon footprint reduction.

Establishing robust mechanisms will foster a comprehensive understanding of the AI development and implementation cycle. Governance should be designed to proceed in parallel with the AI development process and use methodologies and expertise from multiple parties. This means that both AI developers and policymakers must be able to speak the same language.

9.6. AI, HUMANITY AND SOCIAL NETWORK

Artificial intelligence is a powerful new tool that is rapidly changing humanity. AI is changing what it means to be human, the ability to make choices, and the moral implications of various judgments.

Aristotle pointed out that the ability to make practical judgments depends on habit and practice. The emergence of artificial intelligence and machine learning has seen machines replace judgment in everyday applications. Machines pose a potential threat to people and effectively influence the way people make judgments. For example, a bank manager regularly decides which people to hire in different positions, which loans to approve, and other administrative decisions. Now algorithms have replaced human judgment, and these people in management positions no longer have to develop practical judgment.

Machine learning and artificial intelligence have been used to create recommendation engines that have become prevalent intermediaries in the consumption of culture. These recommendation engines limit choice and significantly reduce serendipity by presenting consumers with algorithmically curated options of things to watch, read, stream, and websites to visit later. Human taste is slowly being replaced by machine taste. One advantage is that machines can analyze a wider range of choices than a human may have the time or energy to complete independently. The selection of options by the engines is optimized based on what people have preferred in the past. The major fear is that people's choices will be affected by their history in a new and unforeseen way. We are already seeing a generalization of the echo chamber that people experience with social media.

The widespread emergence of powerful predictive technologies is already disrupting primary political institutions. These technologies violate human rights based on the idea that human beings are majestic, unpredictable, self-directed agents whose freedoms must be guaranteed by the state. Algorithms initially created with good intentions, such as regulating speech on online platforms, have been used to censor speech ranging from religious content to sexual diversity. Artificial intelligence-based technologies and systems created to monitor illegal activities have been used to track and target human rights defenders. In the fields of medicine and security, algorithms that had noble intentions have been used to discriminate against people of color when used to detect cancers or to maliciously assess the flight risk of people accused of crimes. The question is whether political institutions will continue to protect human rights in the same way as predictive technologies influence decision making and humanity.

Self-regulation has done little to help. On the contrary, it has delayed the development and implementation of laws needed to regulate the use of AI and protect human rights.

AI and machine learning will make better decisions, away from the biases that humans usually have, in the not-so-distant future. Humanity is faced with the prospect of losing something vital. Unpredictability is a significant factor in how people understand themselves and what they love about themselves. There is concern that as an AI-mediated world becomes increasingly predictable, humans will eventually lose a significant aspect and become less like previous generations. Companies and governments must commit to designing AI tools, technologies and services that respect human rights and, by extension, human choices by default.

Social networks were also initially lauded for creating connections and bringing people together. However, a study published in the journal Scientific Reports indicates that algorithms worsen existing inequalities and discriminate against specific groups of people. Basically, the study sought to analyze how social mechanisms affect the rank distributions of two of the most popular algorithms. The algorithms chosen are PageRank, an algorithm on which Google's search engine is based, and Who-to-Follow, the algorithm used by

Twitter to suggest people you may find interesting and want to follow. These ranking algorithms have been shown to increase the popularity of already popular users and can lead to a lack of opportunities for specific groups of people.

The researchers sought to understand how these algorithms usually err based on their structure and network characteristics. Using 2,000 people for the study, the researchers simulated different networks and adjusted the social mechanisms of the relationships between individuals in each network. Some of the changes made to the networks included changing the number of minorities, the way active users connected with other users, and the way people associated in general in the network.

The researchers wanted to assess whether people associated more with an already popular individual and whether they were more likely to connect with individuals similar to themselves. The preference to connect with people similar to oneself is a principle known as homophily, which essentially means that birds of the same species associate.

Researchers have found that homophily is the main social mechanism responsible for distorting the visibility of minorities in rankings and the percentage of minorities. Majority groups associate with other members of the majority, which means that minority groups are underrepresented in higher rankings.

Minorities can overcome the challenge of underrepresentation by using a strategic approach when they come into contact with celebrities. These strategic connections will help minorities achieve statistical parity in the top rankings. Statistical parity means that if the number of minorities within a population is 20%, the same should be reflected in the people within a network, especially in the top ranks. It is up to minorities to make more connections with other people in the majority and become more active to increase their visibility in the network. On the other hand, the majority can diversify their connections with minority groups to increase visibility.

Using realistic social networking scenarios, it is evident from the study that ranking algorithms and social recommendation algorithms on social networking platforms such as Twitter can distort the visibility of minority groups in unexpected ways.

It is important that algorithms and other artificial intelligence systems work effectively and efficiently because we are becoming increasingly dependent on these systems.

The three main contributions that sociologists, AI developers and other experts can bring through interdisciplinary collaboration and policy influence are:

- Criticism and politics of refusal- the analysis will help unpack the politics of algorithmic technologies by drawing on existing social theories, expertise and methods. If necessary, society can exercise rejection of algorithmic technologies to dismantle unjust systems and institutions.

- New technologies challenge established systems, which tend to be resistant to change.

- Improving algorithmic governance - Problems of social inequality are issues of public concern and are therefore addressed through institutions charged with safeguarding the public good. Governments have a role to play in facilitating policies and regulations that promote sound algorithmic systems. We can already see that governments around the world have a strong push to rein in the tech giants.

When an AI system is implemented, human intervention is still required. Even for the most AI-inclined organizations, it is necessary to have humans within the loop so as to minimize and avoid risks and maximize the benefits of AI.

Here, there are the roles and impact of human intervention in AI systems:

- AI checks and balances. The importance of humans in the AI cycle is normative, ethical, and reputational. The presence of humans within the AI system helps safeguard inaccurate data that can lead to bad decisions and other negative outcomes. AI system biases can occur during training of the AI model or as trend biases, as the AI system always reacts more to recent activities than to previous actions. An AI system cannot understand the complexities of a moral decision. For example, AI in healthcare shows how AI and humans can work together to improve outcomes. Without human intervention, AI can cause serious harm, especially in decision making. AI advises the physician, who then determines whether the recommended option

is valid.

People must constantly monitor the accuracy and responses of AI to reduce the incidence of defects that could cause harm or catastrophe. Humans have a role to play in constantly training AI models to ensure that they improve. We are already seeing an initiative by major companies using AI to have formal programs in place to monitor their digital reliability.

- Models for human and AI collaboration. Human-in-the-loop (HitL) reinforcement learning and conversational AI are two excellent examples of how human intervention helps AI systems make better decisions.

HitL reinforcement learning allows AI systems to leverage machine learning to learn by observing human behavior in real work and use cases. These systems rely on human feedback and augment human interactions for continuous self-development and continuous improvement. HitL provides a controlled environment that reduces and eliminates the inherent risk of bias and its consequences in decision making. The benefits of the HitL reinforcement learning model are seen especially in industries that produce critical vehicle and aircraft parts, particularly in areas where equipment must meet very high standards. In these special situations, machine learning increases the speed and accuracy of inspections, while human intervention ensures that manufactured parts are safe and secure for passengers.

Conversational artificial intelligence provides near-human communications. It helps lighten the workload of employees by handling the simplest tasks and knowing when to turn more complex issues over to humans for decision making. The best example of this model is contact centers.

Customers request assistance from a contact center through available channels, including calls, texts, or chats with a customer service representative. The virtual agent will listen and understand the customer's needs and engage in a back-and-forth conversation. The virtual agent will use machine learning and artificial intelligence to decide how to proceed and what to do based on what it has learned from previous experiences. Many artificial intelligence systems within contact centers can generate speech to help communicate with the customer and mimic the feeling of a human being typing or talking on the other end.

In most cases, the virtual agent will sufficiently help customers solve their problems. However, there are complex situations where the artificial intelligence system cannot keep typing or talking, so it smoothly transfers to a live representative. The live representative will take over the call or chat and solve the customer's problem. In these scenarios, the AI system can move from automation to augmentation, listening to the conversation and offering recommendations that help the live representative make the best decision.

The combination of conversational AI and cognitive AI can help systems understand the emotional state of the customer on the other end of the line. Other benefits include handling complex dialogues and interactions, providing real-time translations, and adapting to the behavior of the person on the line. Conversational AI with cognitive AI will take human assistance to a higher level of sophistication.

- The blend of automation and human interaction leads to augmented intelligence.

The best applications of AI are seed applications, where AI systems are monitored by people and augment people. In these applications, AI helps people improve their skills, progress through the skill continuum, and empower themselves to take on more complex challenges. The AI system will continuously learn and improve, while being constantly monitored to avoid risks and potentially harmful consequences.

Models as diverse as cognitive AI, conversational AI, and HitL reinforcement learning, combined with real people with expertise, empathy, ingenuity, and moral judgment, will lead to augmented intelligence and increasingly positive outcomes.

10

BLOCKCHAIN, AI & CYBERSECURITY

CHAPTER TEN

BLOCKCHAIN TECHNOLOGY

10.1. BLOCKCHAIN TECHNOLOGY AND ITS EVOLUTION: BAAS, CRYPTOCURRENCY, NFT AND CROSS-CHAIN

Blockchain is a revolutionary technology introduced in 2009. In recent years, blockchain has been extensively tested and used in various industries, in some cases even creating real new markets. In fact, in addition to the hype generated by Bitcoin and other cryptocurrencies, blockchain is turning into a mainstream revolution. Several companies in various industries are working on projects involving blockchain. The financial sector is the most affected as blockchain revolutionizes payments and contracts. A PwC study predicts that blockchain will create 40 million jobs and contribute $1.76 trillion to the global economy.

Blockchain-as-a-Service (Baas)

Blockchain-as-a-service (BaaS) has the potential to impact several industries. BaaS is the creation and third-party management of cloud-

based networks for companies creating blockchain applications. BaaS represents new developments in blockchain and could prove to be the catalyst for widespread adoption of the technology.

BaaS allows users to leverage cloud-based resources to host, build and manage their own blockchain system. Both consumers and businesses are increasingly adopting blockchain technology. BaaS eliminates the overhead and operational complexities associated with creating, configuring, managing and maintaining a blockchain infrastructure, which is a significant barrier. The role of a BaaS provider is quite similar to that of a web hosting provider, where these third-party companies take care of the infrastructure and maintenance. Here, there are some of the most popular uses of blockchain-as-a-service in the world today that are increasing adoption in enterprises.

- Amazon-managed blockchain: The service is designed to facilitate the creation and management of scalable blockchain networks. The service was developed using open source frameworks such as Ethereum and Hyperledger Fabric.

- Microsoft partnered closely with ConsenSys to introduce Ethereum blockchain-as-a-service on Microsoft Azure in 2015.

- R3 is a consortium of global financial institutions that introduced Corda, a distributed financial ledger.

- Bloq offers a wide range of BaaS tools to provide enterprise reconciliation, enterprise security and authentication solutions. The Bloq platform ensures that companies build and customize blockchain technology to meet their specific and current needs. Bloq features particular smart wallets, a smart contracts platform, and a decentralized cloud that helps companies store and manage data.

- LutinX offers an ecosystem of blockchain applications that help companies experiment, iterate and deploy solutions quickly and securely. LutinX uses a hybrid of public and regulated networks to offer up-to-date authentication and immutability standards, focusing on Blockchain for education, intellectual property and traceability. Currently, LutinX represents the only project that integrates multiple market segments with an integrated KYC system - in full compliance with SEC (US) and FINMA (CHE) regulations. In addition, the hybrid system offers a complete AML Blockchain ecosystem that complies with international regulations.

- Factom is known for its two BaaS tools, including Factom Harmony and Factom dLoc. Factom Harmony is a registry tool used to convert documents into a single digitized platform to reduce audit time and costs. Factom dLoc, on the other hand, uses encryption to authenticate and verify personal documents such as birth certificates and property titles.

- Symbiont has created a BaaS platform for fintech companies in different industries. The Symbiont platform is used to verify the origin of documents and transparently records all payments on a ledger for loans and mortgages. Symbiont is also used to protect private documents and reveal ownership of securities in real time from crowdfunding platforms and private equity firms.

- Blockstream's BaaS offers scalable solutions for the Bitcoin ecosystem and protocol. Blockstream's Bitcoin processing software has helped create a large peer-to-peer financial system that eliminates the need for third parties.

- PayStand is another example of BaaS, specializing in sending and receiving payments between businesses. PayStand, through its BaaS, incorporates blockchain into its documentation and payment processes to ensure verifiability and immutability. BaaS installs networks that help authenticate certificates such as deeds, diplomas and receipts. It also has an administration platform that enables in-depth, real-time examination of a user's data. Finally, PayStand helps automate the end-to-end financial process in the areas of accounting, cash management and reconciliation.

- Skuchain's EC3 platform helps companies in the shipping and logistics industry install blockchain-based infrastructure in their current IT processes. Skuchain's ledger enables companies in these industries to simultaneously access a cloud environment, the blockchain protocol and internal applications. BaaS is compatible with most supply chain processes and immediately installs chain-of-custody tools and smart

contracts.

- BlockApps has a permission-based BaaS solution for enterprise customers focused on security. The blockchain development environment is designed to run on a node locally or on the cloud. Implementation of the solutions takes place quickly. The versatility of the BlockApps BaaS platform has enabled the development of blockchain solutions from smart insurance contracts to fraud prevention in ticketing tools.
- Cryptowerk is helping companies create ledger-based tools that protect critical data and create a tamper-proof chain of custody. Cryptowerk's seal is a blockchain API that relies on the ledger to verify the authenticity of data and digital assets. The widespread deployment of BaaS has covered a wide range of industries, from shipping IDs to GPS telemetry and data collection from smart energy meters.
- LeewayHertz provides end-to-end BaaS and offers a full range of blockchain-based services, including blockchain consulting, blockchain
blockchain-based services, including blockchain consulting, hybrid ledger installation, and maintenance. BaaS offers business solutions from concept to installation. LeewayHertz has worked with large companies such as Budweiser, Disney, and 3M through decentralized applications (dApps).
Cryptocurrencies
The cryptocurrency industry has also evolved since the birth of Bitcoin. People remain the primary users of the technology, and trust remains a key element. Cryptocurrencies have yet to obtain the necessary legal status as an investment or store of value in most countries around the world. In addition, many cryptocurrencies are not supported by monetary, legal and institutional structures like traditional financial services. Confidence in cryptocurrencies stems from the technology that supports them. At present, cryptocurrencies have some flaws, such as unpredictability, risk, and volatility. Cryptocurrencies are a peer-to-peer electronic money system designed to eliminate intermediaries such as banks. Cryptocurrencies have disrupted traditional banking systems as users are attracted to their independence and decentralized, non-invasive nature.
The mass adoption of cryptocurrencies will lead to truly decentralized finance. However, this can only be achieved through trusted

intermediaries. Some assistance is needed to help everyone along the way, such as our grandparents, who may not be able to handle private keys, digital wallets, and seed phrases.

Trusted intermediaries are needed to ensure the success of mainstream aspirations of cryptocurrencies and decentralized finance. Trust is a fundamental element underlying all human interaction. For example, we trust doctors' opinions, food served in restaurants, and many other products and services.

In the context of cryptocurrencies, we have to decide who and what to trust. The ordinary world citizen is not an expert on the codes and protocols available in the cryptocurrency space. When choosing to participate in a token, the next course of action is based on what an individual understands. Information is gathered from the people around us about their trust in the organization behind the protocol and whether it is acting in good faith. Now, because of the development of new and disruptive technologies, the way in which and on whom trust is placed has changed. We have seen that people have moved toward placing their trust in algorithms developed by artificial intelligence and machine learning. Studies have revealed that people are more likely to trust technology due to exposure to the technology itself.

The growing trust in blockchain technology and cryptocurrencies has led to the widespread adoption of cryptocurrencies. Adoption rates vary widely across different demographics. Those with the most exposure, such as developers and engineers, are early adopters of cryptocurrencies, while those with the least exposure are late adopters. Therefore, the role of early adopters is to help less exposed people get on board. Creating a kind of monopoly for people with superior technical knowledge would really weaken the promise of democratization of cryptocurrencies.

As a whole, cryptocurrencies also present usability problems for early adopters and people with Internet access. Some of these challenges relate to the management of passwords and private keys. Most people are only used to managing email, search, and social media functions, which means that unfamiliarity is a hindering factor in the usability of cryptocurrencies.

In general, cryptocurrencies are helping to revolutionize the operation of financial systems by giving users control over their assets. It is no longer necessary to rely on banks and other third-party service providers. Power and independence can become a burden for many people who need to ensure the security of their keys and coins. A good number of users have ended up losing their private keys and access to their coins, worth millions of dollars. What should happen is that newcomers to the cryptocurrency space should not be thrown into the abyss and drown. There should be a facilitation process for people to learn how to manage their private keys to be comfortable with managing the keys and their coins. This would also provide simplified access to decentralized finance (DeFi). If users feel confident about what lies ahead, it will herald further growth in the cryptocurrency space. Cryptocurrency exchanges and platforms must focus on education, user experience, and customer support to eliminate trust issues and ensure the prosperity of the entire ecosystem. Platforms and exchanges that engage in educational initiatives and improve user experience stand out from the rest and set themselves on a path to growth. Cryptocurrencies can only reach their true potential in realizing decentralized finance and creating value for people by promoting adoption across all demographics, such as age, gender, education, geographic location, and technical knowledge. The human touch is critical to the widespread adoption of cryptocurrencies, despite the promise of eliminating middlemen.

The degree of transparency and accountability provided by cryptocurrencies is better and cannot be compared to that of a conventional financial institution. Blockchain technology offers a high degree of transparency and accountability, eliminating the need for a trusted central authority to oversee the system. In conclusion, the fundamental properties of blockchain technology facilitate the creation of trust in cryptocurrencies.

The Non-Fungible Tokens (NFTs)

Another area of blockchain is then Non-Fungible Tokens (NFTs), which are digital assets comprising a wide range of unique tangible and intangible items, such as virtual real estate, sports cards, and digital sneakers.

A significant advantage of owning a digital collectible over a physical collectible such as a rare minted coin is that NFTs contain distinctive information that makes them unique and verifiable. This makes the creation and circulation of counterfeit collectibles impossible, as each asset can be traced back to the original issuer.

An NFT cannot be traded directly with another NFT, as they cannot be identical even if they are in the same platform, game or collection. This characteristic distinguishes them from regular cryptocurrencies. They have been likened to festival tickets that carry the name of the event, the name of the buyer, the date of the event, and the venue. It is not possible to exchange one festival ticket for another festival ticket.

A considerable number of NFTs have been constructed using the Ethereum token standards ERC-721 and ERC-1155. These standards represent blueprints created by Ethereum to facilitate the distribution of NFTs and compatibility with the broader ecosystem, including exchanges and wallet services. NFTs are stored in digital wallets as collectibles, and their use is spreading beyond the arts and sports to virtual games and real estate.

Here, there are other notable features of NFTs:

- Non-interoperable: NFTs cannot be used across the board to replace or exchange for another NFT. For example, a CryptoPunk cannot be used in the CryptoKitties game and vice versa. The same applies to collectibles and collectible cards, which cannot be used interchangeably across platforms.

- Indivisible: NFTs cannot be divided into smaller units as is the case with Bitcoins, which can be divided into smaller denominations called satoshi. An NFT will exist only as a whole object. It is not possible to own a part of an NFT.

- Indestructible: Non-fungible tokens cannot be destroyed, replicated or destroyed because all data is stored on the blockchain via smart contracts. The ownership of NFTs is immutable, which means that players and collectors are the true owners of their NFTs and not the companies that created them. Ownership of NFTs is completely different and cannot be compared to buying music from iTunes, where the user does not own what he or she buys. In these scenarios, you only purchase the license to listen to the music and do not own it.

- Verifiable: One of the significant advantages of blockchains is the storage of historical ownership data. Therefore, the ownership of a digital artwork can be traced back to the original creator, which helps authenticate artworks without the need for third-party verification.

NFTs are becoming increasingly popular among cryptocurrency companies and users because they have revolutionized the gaming and collectibles spaces. With the widespread adoption of blockchain technology, investment in NFTs has increased, with players and collectors happy to become immutable owners of game items and other unique assets.

The opportunity to make money from these digital assets is very attractive. Individuals can directly sell their digital assets, which they accumulate by playing, on the secondary market, including avatars, costumes, and in-game currency. Artists are happy to be able to sell their artwork digitally without resorting to galleries and auction houses. The ability to sell directly to a global audience means they

can retain a significant portion of their profits, reducing agent fees and other administrative costs. A substantial advantage of digital assets is that royalties can be programmed directly into the digital artwork, ensuring that the original creator continues to receive a percentage of sales each time the work is sold to a new owner. Some industry players have been able to develop structures and monetize. Examples of systems include virtual casinos and theme parks such as Decentraland and The Sandbox. The value of digital assets follows the rules of supply and demand, just as in other markets. The scarcity of NFTs, combined with high demand from investors, gamers, and collectors, means that people are willing to pay high prices. Many NFTs have made a lot of money for their owners, such as one investor who shelled out $220,000 to buy a segment of the Monaco digital track in the F1 game Delta time. Through the NFT, it receives 5 percent dividends from all races held there.

Digital collectibles, particularly art and sports memorabilia, attract hundreds of thousands of dollars. NFTs have inspired a crypto art movement as more and more people join this craze. For example, NBA Top Shot, a platform by Dapper Labs in collaboration with the basketball league, has attracted huge sales driven by celebrities and sports fans. The rise in interest in tokens comes as bitcoin and other cryptocurrencies have seen big rises.

Non-fungible tokens are expected to transform the fortunes of content creators. They will allow creators to own the property rights to their creations and profit from them in many different ways. Musicians have struggled to make a living from their work in the digital age, and NFTs can help prove ownership of work and create an additional revenue stream from their work. Crypto art has been the fastest growing section of the digital collectibles market. More and more people are looking for native digital asset classes outside of established markets. The NFT market is maturing well and attracting people who have accumulated wealth and reputation and are looking to invest in purely virtual assets. Established digital artists such as Beeple have recently sold their NFT-based artworks through famous auction houses such as Christie's.

NFTs are here to stay, despite the price surge being compared to the speculative cryptocurrency craze. NFTs are strongly advocated as the way to formalize digital ownership and extend ownership beyond the life of any game, company or platform. Many sports franchises, governing bodies and the entertainment industry have shown strong interest in developing NFTs for their hardcore fans. The NBA Top Shot already boasts more than 100,000 active collectors and more than $215 million in sales.

In this way, NFTs represent another disruptive innovation related to Blockchain technology. The world is changing faster, and regulators don't just have to be lawyers or politicians, but also technicians. We are already inside the new digital world, and clear rules need to be applied to the international system before corruption and crisis arrive. Like any opportunity, risks are outside the door.

Cross-chains

Staying with the blockchain theme, then one cannot fail to mention cross-chains, namely the interoperability between two independent blockchains. Basically, cross-chains support the transmission of information and value between different blockchain networks. Blockchain and distributed ledger networks continue to explode every day, making it necessary to interconnect new chains as people find different applications for the latest technology. Most blockchain networks operate in isolated ecosystems to meet a unique set of needs.

Initially, blockchains were considered a complete solution for all transactions, contracts and anything else undertaken on the single chain. However, the challenges associated with innovation and scalability revealed that the technology was not as practical as initially imagined. The fact that blockchains operate in isolation severely limited the full fruition of ledger technology. A good example is the inability to share information between Bitcoin and Ethereum, two of the most popular blockchains. Users cannot enjoy the full benefits of ledger technology because of the handicap of establishing communication between different blockchain technologies.

In the proliferation of projects, blockchains, ledgers and DAGs have been used to perform a whole range of interactions and data processing functions. Other blockchains have been designed for community organizations, religions, government departments and unions. These developments have led to the emergence of different

types of chains and the growing need for cross-chain technology to solve interoperability problems. Cross-chain technology facilitates accessible communication between blockchains and seamless information sharing.

Interoperability refers to the concept in which blockchains can communicate with each other to enable smooth information sharing. It is the ability to see and access information contained or stored in a different blockchain. This means that if information is sent to another blockchain, a user on the other side can see it, read it, understand it and react appropriately using minimal effort throughout the process. Cross-chain technology seeks to create and improve interoperability between blockchains, thus eliminating the need for third parties to establish such a connection.

Blockchain interoperability will help preserve the decentralized nature of blockchain technology. Third parties represent centralized systems, which are the antithesis of decentralized blockchain technology. The elimination of intermediaries or third parties will enable communication between decentralized blockchains and herald a return to fully decentralized systems.

In general, cross-chain interactions are classified into isomorphic cross-chains and heterogeneous cross-chains, depending on the underlying technology.

- Isomorphic cross-chains: The characteristics of these cross-chains, including the consensus algorithm, security mechanism, network topology and block generation verification logic, are relatively consistent and the interaction between them is simple.

- Heterogeneous cross-chains: Cross-chain interactions are quite complex and use the PoW algorithm commonly used for Bitcoin and the PBFT consensus algorithm widely used for Tendermint. The composition of the blocks and the deterministic guarantee mechanism are distinctly different, which makes it difficult to design a direct interaction between chains. Interaction between heterogeneous chains typically requires the ancillary services of a third party.

Among the early adopters of cross-chain technology is Ripple, which has explored the possibility of cross-chain transactions. The Ripple project aims to make it possible for both institutions and individuals to transfer and exchange digital assets across different blockchains. Ripple wants to become a leader in facilitating cross-chain transactions, closely following its leading role in helping banks settle cross-border payments in other currencies and cryptocurrencies.

Otherwise, new emerging projects are gaining exciting market share, such as the LutinX project.

The identification of open protocols that support universal communication between different blockchains and the introduction of different functionalities will open up possibilities. Interoperability will present opportunities such as multi-token transactions, payments on multiple blockchains, and interaction between different NFT management systems. These functions are the future of the new digital economy and mass adoption of blockchain technology.

10.2. BLOCKCHAIN APPLIED IN THE FOOD INDUSTRY: SUPPLY CHAIN TRACEABILITY

Traceability has become a key tool for the implementation and operation of standards and regulations, increasing transparency in food supply chains. Simply put, traceability is about following a product from production to consumption.

A traceability system refers to the set of data and operations that maintain the required information about a product and its ingredients throughout the production and use chain. The system collects and records data as a product transits from one market participant to another along the chain. The data are used to track in real time and ex post the movement of the product through the value chain, from origin to final destination. Traceability systems vary widely in sophistication and scope. Some methods work to collect data from the entire production chain, while others record data from only part of the production chain. Another difference is between farm-level systems that capture information from a single supply chain and multi-stakeholder traceability platforms that track products across an entire food system. Blockchain is finding wide application in food traceability systems to improve food safety monitoring and enable public and private sector stakeholders to verify that food products meet regulatory requirements and market standards. The technology will help get quick responses from regulators and industry stakeholders if food safety violations are detected. Not only that, the technology will help food growers, processors and packers create cross-border synergies and the transparency needed to access regional and global markets.

Traceability is about the safety of food trade, and its main goal is to reduce contamination, spoilage and illness along the food supply chain. Potential hazards can be identified before affected products enter consumer markets. If an unsafe food passes through the cords and enters the supply system, regulators and other market participants will be able to isolate the product and identify the source. Rapid identification and isolation of products will help prevent adverse consequences. In addition, traceability ensures that affected foods are effectively recalled without distorting the market or causing unnecessary waste when a product is recalled. Traceability is critical for fresh and perishable food value chains, as they are the most susceptible to contamination and spoilage. Examples of these foods include dairy products, meat, vegetables and fruits, where health considerations are a top priority. Implementing end-to-end traceability systems is expensive and challenging. Since the advent of traceability, it has been driven primarily by the private sector. Investment in traceability systems has been driven by factors such as consumer demands, improved efficiency, standards compliance, and risk reduction.

Developing countries have more difficulty in establishing traceability due to lack of technological and physical infrastructure, fragmented informal value chains, and many other challenges. The use of distributed ledger technology in traceability proves to be a masterstroke in circumventing these challenges in developing countries. Blockchain, along with mobile Internet connectivity, is having a positive impact on agricultural supply chains. Mobile Internet connectivity is becoming a critical factor for many traceability systems.

The creation of robust traceability systems supported by blockchain will also bring transformative changes in food traceability and open up international markets. We see its application in the current proof-of-origin and accountability system, such as single-origin coffee, sustainably grown and harvested seafood, and zero-deforestation food production, with immense benefits to local communities. Blockchain is not only an acceptable technology across borders, it is also eliminating middlemen within supply chains, which means these local communities get the most value for their products and hard work.

Blockchain technology provides the advanced technological and recording capabilities required by traceability systems that serve small-scale market needs. Adoption of this technology promotes faster integration of small-scale producers into regional and global supply chains, regardless of their location in the world. Food Trust, IBM's blockchain-based traceability platform, currently works with 80 retailers and suppliers, including large retail and food giants such as Carrefour, Nestle and Walmart. More and more pilot projects, such as FoodLogiQ, Provenance, and LuteniX, are being developed and piloted around the world, in Africa, Asia, and Asia, to facilitate access to export markets for small farmers through traceability.

Lastly, blockchain and all other DLTs are transforming the way

transactions are conducted and promoting greater transparency. Accredited data in blockchain-supported traceability systems are verified by consensus and updated in real time among system actors. Information is stored permanently without alteration.
In general, blockchain like all emerging traceability technologies can transform the following four areas of the food system:

- Consumer demand for transparency in food production. Consumers are increasingly demanding greater transparency in the food system to avoid illegal, counterfeit and unethical products. Greater clarity will help inform the decision to purchase a product. Data on products will prove useful for consumers who want to know everything that has been produced, including whether they are antibiotic-free, organic, or locally produced. The use of various technologies, including Blockchain, will help with in-depth tracking of supply chain data, as labels and certifications alone may not be sufficient for transparency. Blockchain technologies will prove useful in minimizing and ultimately preventing food fraud. Food fraud is the intentional adulteration of food for profit and can include dilution, substitution, misrepresentation, and counterfeiting of ingredients, whole foods, and packaging. Food fraud is estimated to cost about $40 billion and is associated with public health risks, loss of consumer trust and market inefficiencies. A combination of Blockchain and automated data capture through IoT devices will help solve fraud problems, protect human populations, and meet consumer demand for transparency.

- Improve the ability to prevent, identify and respond to food safety problems. According to the World Health Organization, 1 in 10 people get sick from food contamination. Food safety problems are a huge burden on public health and the economy. Food traceability through blockchain technology will help governments and stakeholders identify, isolate and respond effectively to food safety problems. It will facilitate practical inspections throughout the value chain and reduce the cost of recalls. Although food traceability will not eliminate food-borne illnesses, it will significantly reduce exposure to foodborne outbreak risks through faster and more efficient identification of the exact source of contamination. The use of distributed ledger and IoT technologies will protect the health of consumers and protect all actors in the food system from financial losses. For example, a Walmart pilot project revealed that blockchain could help companies identify the origin of food products and items. It was possible to trace the origin of a mango in just 2.2 seconds, compared to an average of

seven days with standard procedures. Traceability will ensure that only contaminated food products are removed from the shelves and not other products.

- Improve supply chain optimization and prevent food loss: More than 1.3 billion tons of food is wasted, accounting for one-third of all food production. Emerging technologies, such as blockchain, will help address supply chain inefficiencies at several stages, including post-harvest, processing, and distribution. Addressing food loss will reduce procurement and distribution costs, which will eventually be passed on to consumers. Traceability technologies make it easier to identify sources of food loss and provide opportunities for increased supply chain automation, real-time collection of data needed for decision making, and faster scanning and ordering of products. All of these measures improve the speed at which food moves through the supply chain, effectively reducing spoilage. Traceability will also lead to incremental changes in food supply chains to improve sustainability and meet future food demand.

- Validate source claims and support sustainability goals. Food systems have far-reaching social and environmental impacts. Food systems are responsible for 25 percent of global greenhouse gas emissions, deforestation and 70 percent of freshwater withdrawals. Emerging food traceability technologies embrace the multifaceted approach needed to address sustainability challenges. While traceability will certainly support global sustainability goals, it cannot fully manage the environmental footprint of food systems.
In conclusion, different models can be used to implement food traceability and target each of these impact areas in the food system. However, all of these impact areas are not mutually exclusive, and

traceability models, such as those using Blockchain, can achieve the desired effects across the board. Blockchain offers a multidisciplinary approach to food traceability and, as the technology matures, can provide end-to-end traceability at scale.

10.3. BLOCKCHAIN IN THE EDUCATION SECTOR

The most important areas where blockchain is expected to transform the education sector are:

- Student records and accreditation. Blockchain is considered the perfect technology for storing, using and tracking student credentials. For example, diplomas issued via blockchain will allow students to conveniently and quickly access their records and make it easier for them to share their qualifications with potential employers. The system eliminates the need for employers to contact universities and colleges to verify information about a candidate's achievements. Another significant benefit is that their records are not locked up in their alma mater, but belong completely to the student. Students will be able to use their data at any time or when needed.
Blockchain offers a way out to streamline verification procedures and minimize fraudulent incidents related to academic credentials, making it more efficient.
In Europe, many universities and colleges are partnering with Lirax. Org, a software startup that has launched a Blockcerts toolset that essentially provides an open infrastructure for creating, issuing, displaying and verifying blockchain-based certificates.
- A partnership platform. Blockchain as a platform provides transparent storage of records and supports sharing and communication. Universities and colleges strive to ensure that students have a successful experience during their studies. It is about building a relationship between professors and students by providing appropriate guidance and advice, without intermediaries. The platform can share information, including lectures and important events, which can help support efficient relationships between faculty, students and alumni. Blockchain will help break down potential barriers between students and faculty.
In this regard, a digital badge can be used to communicate and verify specific skills acquired. The technology can assemble multiple badges in one place, allowing users to generate a passport that students/graduates can share with potential employers. Indorse uses blockchain to verify e-portfolios: users upload claims, often with a

verification link used by other users to verify the claim.
- Copyright protection. Academic institutions face the challenge of plagiarism, management and dissemination of copyrighted material, especially on the Internet. Blockchain technology offers a secure form of storage, as information is recorded in an unalterable and encrypted state. Therefore, academic material will not only be secure but also immutable. Any use of the material will be recorded on the chain, so the owner will be able to control access to his or her intellectual property. With blockchain technology, ownership can be easily verified and the use of intellectual and digital property can be tracked.

- In Human Resources. Blockchain technology can streamline and simplify processes for all parties, both students and employees. It can simplify the student application process, job applications and personal data storage. Blockchain makes it possible to store and share student information and certifications. As pointed out earlier, all information is protected through advanced security features and protocols, making it impossible to falsify data. Employees and human resource managers are guaranteed access to and use of accurate and relevant information. There will be no more lies and inconsistencies about degrees and diplomas, achievements, and institutions attended, and it will no longer be necessary to verify all this information for accuracy.
Not only that, educational institutions, especially higher education institutions, have great human resources, in addition to checking educational qualifications, work history and background checks. Again, many of these activities are highly manual and time-consuming. Streamlining these processes through DLT will help human resource workers do more work efficiently and faster. Large educational institutions, such as universities, will benefit immensely from adopting DLT in hiring to conduct background checks and verify work history.
- Driving and supporting innovation. An important application of blockchain in the education sector is the development of learning platforms. One such project is the Education Ecosystem platform, which uses blockchain technology to facilitate connections between academics, developers, students and content producers. Using similar principles, educational institutions can create their own ecosystems that enable access to study materials and the sharing of projects and

ideas for students.

Internally generated tokens can be used to request study materials, download books and request feedback. Tokens are earned by users through inviting new participants, watching videos and submitting contributions. Content creators also receive rewards for their materials and activities, and users earn tokens by interacting with their content. The net effect is that students have access to more educational materials, the more they learn and practice. Interactions on educational platforms have clear benefits for all stakeholders and improve outcomes overall.

Such tokens represent actual personalized cryptocurrencies. A cryptocurrency platform can use a student payment method and process payments that can involve students, governments, financial institutions, and scholarship agencies. There are higher education institutions that are already using Bitcoin (BTC) as a form of payment. King's College of New York is one such university that has accepted bitcoin and, in the process, eliminated credit card transaction fees. It is a great example of how digital assets can be used in the industry. I think this kind of market should be used to support students within a complementary circuit where a closed currency can be used next to the official currency. In this way, the value of educational offerings will be preserved and those who achieve better results and stand out in their studies will have access to more benefits.

- Disruptive business models - While the adoption of blockchain in higher education has focused on record keeping and improving efficiency, the real power of the technology is the creation of new business models.

One such disruptive business model has been adopted by Woolf University, which aims to become a borderless institution powered by blockchain. The university plans to use blockchain and smart contracts as the basis of the relationship between faculty and students.

If successful, the new educational platform can become disruptive - lowering tuition fees, automating administrative tasks and reducing overhead, increasing faculty pay, and securing records for faculty and students. Lecturers can choose to be paid in their local currency or in Woolf tokens.

The open-source university model would allow students to benefit from standardized educational opportunities regardless of their location in the world. Blockchain would offer a reasonably priced one-stop shop for different courses and a unified blockchain database to store verifiable credentials.

These transformations, in some cases, are already realities. The Ministry of Education and Training in Vietnam recently signed an exclusive agreement with a Singapore-based smart contract platform to store student data using blockchain. The result of the trial was the creation of a transparent and immutable record that helps speed up verification processes. Certification management can be solved quickly using technology that will have a transformative effect on education and become cost-effective. Identity verification and record keeping are critical applications of blockchain technology that can be leveraged and used in the education sector. Vietnam's student repository represents the first and most significant application of public blockchain at the national level by a country's government. After the trial period, the national qualification repository program will be implemented for new steps.

Of course it is still to be considered that many universities have failed to see the potential of blockchain in daily operations. Most top universities remain conservative in their approach and hesitate to embrace new technologies to better serve the needs of education, research and students. The higher education industry is complex and is characterized by established traditions, norms and positions. Traditions and historians are major obstacles to innovation and adoption of new technologies. Innovators and companies hoping to disrupt the higher education sector will need to take this reality into account.

Blockchain in education offers turnkey opportunities, future developments and a green field of business opportunities. The higher education sector is characterized by few serious blockchain providers and little interest from would-be buyers. Higher education policymakers need to work with stakeholders to explore different ways to address the above challenges. At the same time, they need to support the internet infrastructure needed to deploy and support blockchain technology.

Universities have many different ways to exclude competitors, and they have succeeded. Despite the presence of massive open online courses (MOOCs) and low-cost online universities, these options have not yet surpassed the value of high-level, brick-and-mortar university education and facilities. The biggest challenge blockchain technology faces is disrupting the EduTech space.

However, blockchain offers new education and research practices, greater access to investors, peer-to-peer education models, and other emerging uses such as citizen science.

10.4. THE LEGALITY OF BLOCKCHAIN TECHNOLOGY AND CRYPTOCURRENCY

The potential of blockchain is so vast that just what is currently happening may only be scratching the surface. Blockchain continues to optimize processes and develop new services as its potential and application are widely understood. Government adoption of blockchain is the obstacle preventing the technology from becoming mainstream. However, some countries have taken significant steps toward creating enabling laws and regulations to support the incorporation of blockchain into systems and processes. Blockchain can help the public service reduce bureaucratic barriers, improve efficiency, promote information sharing, and accelerate automation through smart contracts. Many countries around the world have created digital strategies related to the deployment of blockchain in different sectors. Laws and regulations aim to support rather than stifle the widespread adoption of blockchain.

Here, there are some of the most popular applications of blockchain of a legal nature: - Smart Contract. Blockchain allows for the secure storage of digital information and real-time sharing with relevant parties. In addition, all stored data is easily verifiable to avoid fraud and eliminate the need for drawing up contracts in a courtroom setting. Data stored on the blockchain is immutable and removes all concerns of tampered documents. Smart contracts execute themselves following the meeting or completion of set criteria. It essentially means that you cannot move to the next transaction without completing the previous one on the ledger.

- Document notarization. We are seeing more start-ups deploy document notarization through blockchain. The basic idea is to provide proof that a particular document existed at a specific point in time in an independently verifiable manner.

Timestamping offers a breakthrough in blockchain notarization, including digital signatures, digital authentication, and other applications. Any digital data can be timestamped for a start, and anyone who has possession of original content with a digital timestamp can authenticate it without the need for any proof of authenticity or third- party notary.

Some of the benefits to using blockchain technology for notary public services include:

- Security of stored documents and deeds.
- Private key access to the papers.
- Secured storage on the blocks alongside appropriate timestamps.
- Seamless transfer of document ownership through the network.
- Open transactions on the web for the verification process.

A significant legal risk involved is that calendar and time are not legally considered as proof authentication. Thus, time alone cannot be used to prove the authority of a document, but it needs to be used alongside proof of issuer and authenticity.

- Intellectual rights. Blockchain technology provides a ledger for intellectual property owners in a similar manner to notarization. Owners of intellectual rights such as arts, lyrics, music, and inventions can set up smart contracts to control the terms of use for various items and the type of remuneration that accompanies their use.
Blockchain offers the opportunity to quickly resolve copyright cases. For example, the concept would see an end to high-profile cases that involve music artists being accused of stealing song riffs from other musicians or record labels.

- Legal issue. Proper governance and regulation are significant hurdles facing blockchain technology, just like any other emerging technology. However, it's different for various countries depending on the general stance of emerging technologies and the path each nation seeks to chart/explore.
The ability of blockchain to cross jurisdictional boundaries is a major issue cited by governments. The fact that nodes on a blockchain can be located anywhere worldwide may pose complex jurisdictional problems. That means that every transaction would be subject to

the laws applicable in the location of each node in the network.

The principles of contract and title would change across the different jurisdictions presenting a unique challenge. That would mean that the decentralized nature of blockchain would be greatly limited in the cumbersome way it would have to comply with legal and regulatory regimes. Blockchain technology, in its very nature, is predicated on multiple users continuously contributing to the chain. Even now, in the early adoption stages, players and users in the blockchain industry must always be aware of legal issues or the legal ramifications of deploying a solution. The deployment of blockchain technology may touch different areas of law, including criminal law, regulatory laws, private law, and public law.

Some countries such as the USA, Canada, Australia, England, Australia, Switzerland, India, Germany, Mexico, Italy, Estonia, and France have moved with speed to issue blockchain strategies and roadmaps to realize the full potential of blockchain technology. The strategies have sought to identify and enact effective, efficient. Appropriate regulations and standards, identify skills that will drive further innovation in blockchain and seek enhanced international collaboration and investment.

For example, Australia has even created the Inter-Government Ledger through the Australian Border Force to facilitate the electronic sharing of import/export documentation. The move is meant to verify shipments and to smoothen trade flow. In Germany, blockchain technology is seen as a digital transformation tool in its Blockchain strategy of the Federal Government. As a result, it has become a hub for innovation, distribution, and technology investment.

The National Development and Reform Commission in China seeks blockchain and other technologies as the underpinning technologies to its IT systems. Further steps have been taken through the Blockchain Services Network to facilitate faster, easier and cheaper development of blockchain applications for enterprise users around the world.

However, if we talk about blockchain it is not a given that we are also talking about cryptocurrencies. Indeed, especially at the legal level, cryptocurrencies operate in a systemic legal vacuum in most jurisdictions around the world.

On the brighter side, virtual currencies are heralding global economic and socio-political reforms. Governments world over have been trailing in the attempt to shape an optimal legal platform and regulations in which blockchain and cryptocurrencies can exist. The initial general stance of most governments was negative - with a view that cryptocurrencies were a direct assault on legal currencies. Through blockchain technology, users can confirm transactions

eliminating the need for a central certifying authority such as a central bank. The continued rise of the value and popularity of cryptocurrencies has made it difficult for nations and regulatory authorities to ignore them.

There has been increased scrutiny on virtual currencies and blockchain as governments seek to address matters of jurisdiction and fraud. Most regulatory authorities are closely monitoring the development of blockchain and the cryptocurrency industries.

There has been talk about the development of international policies and how it can be beneficial to certain countries and even world markets. Questions of jurisdiction, national capital control, fraud, terrorism, and money laundering are major talking points in creating legal structure and regulations. Blockchain poses a threat to global markets due to its deregulated nature. Investors will shy off from adopting or deploying blockchain if the industry falls in the gray areas of the law in the specific country.

Countries have made attempts at legal regulation of blockchain and particularly cryptocurrencies. For example, some states are introducing blockchain regulation directly or indirectly to regulate the process of issuing, circulation, and taxation of cryptocurrencies. In other scenarios, some countries have banned blockchain since they have no control over the deployment and development of the technology.

Direct regulations are when governments or mandated regulatory bodies officially introduce a law to govern blockchain-related technology. The indirect regulations require that blockchain companies follow the general rules imposed on tech companies and financial institutions, especially for crypto exchanges.

There are international regulations already in place, such as the European Union General Data Protection Regulation that mandates blockchain companies to conform to the applicable anonymity and data security regulations.

Blockchain technology is legal in the US, the UK, Australia, Japan, Singapore, UAE, and several other countries worldwide. Many other countries are monitoring the development of the blockchain industry without taking active steps to legalize it or criminalize it. However, some regulators have warned their citizens about the risks associated with the acquisition and use of cryptocurrencies.

The United States of America has the most advanced blockchain and cryptocurrency industry. Blockchain and cryptocurrencies have been deployed in day-to-day operations and activities in the business and corporate worlds. Regulations have been put in place to support the further growth of blockchain. For example, cryptocurrency trading is subject to taxation and other tax regulations. In addition, all American cryptocurrency exchanges must verify their clients as per the law. Existing laws and regulations make the USA one of the best countries in the world for the development of blockchain and cryptocurrency industries. However, a few legal challenges exist due to the peculiarities of its tiered government structures - federal law and state law and a lack of common position among regulators.

The development of the national cryptocurrency market in Canada is well ahead of other countries. For example, Canada has developed a digital version of the Canadian dollar to understand blockchain technology better. In addition, cryptocurrency exchanges are registered with the Financial Transactions and Reports Analysis Center of Canada and are thus required to comply with legislation on countering laundering proceeds from crime. Belarus is yet another country that has a robust regulatory framework for the blockchain industry. The blockchain industry is designated as a particular sector that has a different tax and legal regime. As a result, blockchain companies are free to operate from the HTP, Belarus's equivalent of Silicon Valley, and even enjoy tax breaks.

Australia offers favorable conditions for the development of blockchain and cryptocurrency industries. Cryptocurrency activity is not subject to licensing since it isn't considered a financial product. Transactions are subject to ordinary income and corporate taxes, whereas investments in cryptocurrency attract a capital gains tax.

In Norway, Finland and Germany, cryptocurrencies are subject to capital gains tax and wealth tax. Digital currencies are considered a financial instrument in Bulgaria and are subject to applicable income taxes. The tax authorities in Austria treat cryptocurrencies as an intangible asset - their receipt is treated as an operating activity.

In the UK, favorable laws have been passed, making it a leader in cryptocurrency integration. Cryptocurrencies are not subject to UK Money Laundering Regulations. The government is continually working towards normalizing the use of cryptocurrencies.

In other countries such as China, cryptocurrencies are heavily restricted. China offers immense support for its blockchain industry and cryptocurrencies without totally criminalizing the holding of bitcoins. On the other hand, India has banned its banks from dealing in cryptocurrencies which drastically changes the overall legal status of these coins.

10.5. BLOCKCHAIN FUTURE

Staying on the topic of legality, if one were to take a look at the future of blockchain, the regulatory system would be the key to its next phase of development.

Blockchain technology continues its development and widespread adoption towards a decentralized internet. It heralds the rise of Web 3.0 characterized by decentralized finance and only compared to the advent of the internet itself. The revolution has been likened to the beginning of the internet. True success for blockchain technology will be based on proper regulation.

Regulatory bodies need to evolve with the rapidly occurring changes in blockchain technology and the crypto markets. We have seen people take up very opposite positions on the matter of regulation. Some people believe that decentralized technology and law are mutually exclusive. A lack of regulation is not a good thing for the industry, and its meteoric growth is attracting the attention of regulators globally.

Regulators and policymakers worldwide are focused on decentralized finance (DeFi), stablecoins, smart contracts, NFTs, crypto assets, central bank digital assets, and non-hosted wallets. Some innovators are opposed entirely to the idea of regulation, while others propose that the right way to regulate crypto must be found.

Current regulation in the IT industry is not suited for crypto and blockchain since it may ruin the core principles of decentralized technologies. However, there is a realization that both decentralization and regulation are inevitable. The best approach is for regulators and innovators to work together to chart a path forward. In order to find the right balance, the blockchain community requires a more profound and closer working relationship between both regulators and innovators. Initiating dialogue between the blockchain community and regulators and authorities will make it possible to find the right way to regulate the industry — through smart regulation. Otherwise, ruining the core principles of decentralized technologies would return us to the starting point.

Will blockchain and crypto lose their core values with the inception of regulations, or will regulations adapt to the decentralized technology and its immense benefits for society? For a start, the blockchain industry should accept that no inherent aspect of the technology can go wholly unregulated. On the other hand, the technology cannot be overly regulated or banned because it's new and embodies decentralization.

New technologies that cause a significant disruption tends to attract a regulatory crackdown. The distributed ledger technology heralds a new paradigm, such as through decentralized finance (DeFi).

There are numerous approaches being taken around the world to regulate blockchain and cryptocurrency. Countries such as Bermuda, El Salvador, Portugal, Singapore and Ukraine have passed legislation that embraces the decentralized nature of blockchain. Other countries, such as India, Nigeria and Turkey, have banned the technology. Another group of countries, mainly in the Americas and Europe, are at the inflection point. The issue is no longer the introduction of regulation, but how the law will take shape.

Regulators are on a learning curve about blockchain technology. Regulatory frameworks usually are developed incrementally and are designed for centralized and intermediated sectors. For example, DeFi is not vertical and intermediated like traditional finance but takes a flat and peer-to-peer format. In terms of regulation, financial regulations are all about regulating the activities of intermediaries. For DeFi, the lack of intermediaries means that there's no jurisdictional hook. The absence of clear jurisdiction is what makes regulators jittery about a decentralized future associated with blockchain technology.

Governments and regulators have been taken by surprise by blockchain innovations cropping up each day. It's not helped by the decentralized, disintermediated, and borderless nature of blockchain networks. Without a doubt, countries that have embraced blockchain and cryptocurrency are already reaping the rewards. These countries have become the global blockchain technology hubs as investors are attracted to stable regulatory environments. The regulators in these countries realized the value of blockchain technology and acknowledged its benefits. The regulations put in place are carefully considered and have been adapted to blockchain and its decentralized nature. As the technology matures, so will the regulatory approaches to it.

Innovators in the blockchain and cryptocurrency spaces have been opposed to being regulated for fear of being forced into frameworks that don't fit the industry. However, widespread recognition is that decentralization is here to stay, and the regulatory framework is about safeguarding gains and markets. The blockchain industry must explain how the technology is different and why so that policymakers know the benefits and risks associated with its widespread adoption. For example, regulations are being used in crypto, especially for exchanges that offer crypto- to-fiat, such as the Know Your Customer and Anti-Money Laundering laws. Besides the limited rules being used in the blockchain industry, decentralized networks provide greater visibility than traditional finance. Processes and transactions in conventional finance are opaque, preventing visibility across an

entire financial sector.

The introduction of smart regulation in the blockchain industry will drive faster adoption and innovation within the sector. The growth of innovation is on an exponential trajectory. The entry of governments in digital currencies through central bank digital currencies (CDBCs) allows for visibility into the industry and programming of fees and taxes. The elimination of ambiguity in regulation will foster growth, further innovation, and attract investors. Adapting to rules will be necessary for any business in the blockchain industry that wants to operate globally.

In addition to regulatory efforts, blockchain technology and its community is making additional efforts to "go green." Climate change has become a central element of modern business. It is a long-term challenge of the modern era that forces organizations to realign their business models to adapt to the new environmental way of thinking. Cryptocurrencies and other digital assets are pushing to become mainstream industries and must follow environmental and sustainability standards. Crypto mining has become a potential environmental disaster with a single BTC transaction consuming more than 2,264 kWh worth of electricity.

Investors place more value on companies that emphasize environmental, social, and governance principles (ESG). Organizations have signed the Crypto Climate Accord to achieve net-zero emissions by 2030. Several factors affect the sustainability and environmental impact of a cryptocurrency and blockchain project including energy sources powering mining operations, the validation system in use, and how much physical equipment is required.

New and existing blockchain projects are exploring options such as migrating to less energy- intensive validation systems and migrating to renewable energy-based mining to address sustainability and

environmental goals.
- Adopting Newer Crypto Mining Models. Crypto mining refers to the process by which cryptocurrencies are accepted into circulation. It's also how a network confirms new transactions on the distributed blockchain ledger. Sophisticated hardware is used for mining by solving complex computations. The miner earns new tokens and gets paid.
One major disadvantage of mining is the massive amount of energy that is used and the resulting carbon footprint and environmental impact. The traditional method is called "proof of work (PoW)" in which miners compete to solve complex mathematical computations. The consensus requires huge computational power hence increased energy use and emissions. Green crypto mining uses a new model called "proof of stake (PoS)" and has a new set of rules used to validate crypto transactions. It has been a redefinition of how blockchain nodes agree on the accuracy of transactions. The nodes commit "stakes" of tokens in exchange for a chance to be chosen to produce the next block of transactions. Ethereum is perhaps one of the most prominent examples of a leading cryptocurrency project that is transitioning from PoW to a PoS system, intending to reduce its overall energy consumption by 99.95%. The advantage of the POS model includes a lower barrier of entry due to simple hardware requirements and energy efficiency.

- Green Energy Sources. Environmental policies continue to weigh heavier on investors' decision-making processes. Additionally, regulators are increasing their focus on crypto energy use. It has led to a major push toward the use of greener energy sources for the mining process. There are increasing financial incentives to improve the carbon footprint of blockchain and the cryptocurrency ecosystem. Crypto miners are finding solutions by using 100% renewable energy sources or a mix that has a greater amount of renewable energy to reduce their carbon footprint. Solar, geothermal, and wind power are excellent renewable energy sources used to power crypto mining. A few companies are planning to invest huge sums in renewable energy plants dedicated to mining albeit the risk of some cryptocurrencies not justifying the financial outlays. Repurposed power raises heated debates on whether it qualifies as renewable energy. Companies such as Crusoe Energy and Equinor have renovated unused conventional power plants or used excess gas from drilling that would have been burned off. Critics believe that it does get rid of harmful emissions but transfers them to a different industry.

- Handling e-Waste. Blockchain networks present the big challenge

of e-waste from legacy mining operations. The industry grapples with what to do with all the equipment, specialized or not, used for crypto mining. However, alternative validation methods reduce the demand for newer and larger mining rigs in the future reducing the amount of waste produced. Some of the newer cryptocurrencies are mined using renewable energy and alternative validation methods to reduce carbon footprint and environmental impact.

• Cardano is a PoS cryptocurrency built on a peer-reviewed blockchain. People buy units of Cardano to become members of the network instead of mining new coins reducing energy consumption massively.

• Stellar is an energy-efficient blockchain network associated with the cryptocurrency lumen (XLM). Stellar utilizes a consensus mechanism – a group of trusted nodes to authenticate transactions – that operates faster than proof-of-work and proof-of- stake. The network allows people to trade fiat and cryptocurrencies as well as send remittance payments without high fees and lengthy transaction times.

• Nano is another low-energy crypto that is based on "blockchain lattice" technology that creates user blockchains for everyone on the Nano network. Nano uses Open Representative Voting (ORV) where representatives voted in by members of the network act as validators reducing energy consumption.

• Hedera Hashgraph processes transactions in parallel instead of linearly making it comparatively faster than Bitcoin and other legacy cryptocurrencies. With the ability to process up to 100,000 transactions per second, it can rival payment processors like Visa. The Hedera network supports other sustainability projects like their Power Transition energy tracking software.

• Gridcoin utilizes power from idle computers connected to its network for scientific research under the Berkeley Open Infrastructure for Network Computing (BOINC). It uses PoS with validators rewarded with a proof-of-research algorithm.
Blockchain is here to stay implying that ethical choices must be made to ensure a sustainable future. The next generation of blockchain-based solutions will be greener and more sustainable. It calls for creativity from developers in delivering green blockchain solutions

based on new operation and business models, energy efficiency, and the use of renewable energy sources. We can already see new initiatives that are geared toward improving the industry's environmental credentials. Achieving sustainability goals will make cryptocurrencies and blockchain projects more attractive to a wide range of users.

CONCLUSIONS

BLOCKCHAIN, AI & CYBERSECURITY

In this work we have traveled a journey that was first undertaken by the author himself. Yes: we are not saying anything strange in stating how the author has embarked on a fascinating journey through the evolution and challenges posed by artificial intelligence, facial recognition, 5G technology and the blockchain. Through in-depth analysis and a holistic perspective, the book examines the impact of these innovations on society, the economy and the environment, highlighting the opportunities and concerns arising from them.

Ethical and privacy issues, the importance of collaboration between governments, companies and innovators, and the need to adopt sustainable and environmentally friendly solutions are recurring themes throughout the book. The author underlines the importance of a balanced vision, which takes into account the potential of new technologies, but also the challenges they pose.

The reader absolutely cannot escape. The reader is invited to reflect on the implications of these emerging technologies and their role in shaping the future of society. It is essential that all actors involved work together to ensure that technological innovations bring shared benefits and are used responsibly, always keeping ethical, social and environmental issues in mind.

The author hopes that this book can be seen as a valuable resource for anyone wishing to better understand the dynamics that are shaping our technological world and the changes that result from it. With a clear vision of emerging trends and the strategies required to successfully address them, the reader will be better equipped to navigate the ever-changing landscape of technology and its intersections with society.

You are - we are - all invited to answer the call.

9 798865 158950